MY PRETTY VENICE

Isabella Campagnol
Elisabeth Rainer

MY PRETTY VENICE

A Girl's Guide to True Venice

Illustrations by Beatrice Campagnol

GREMESE

*dedicated to Camilla, Costanza, Marta,
Mattia, Fabrizio, Lorenzano and Pier*

Original title
My Pretty Venice
2015 © Gremese International

Drawings by
Beatrice Campagnol

Edited and translated from the Italian by
Sandra Eiko Tokunaga

Photo credits
All photos by Lorenzano Di Renzo except the following:
© Frédéric Prochasson – Fotolia.com (pp.8,9); © Marina e Susanna Sent (pp.18,19, 20); © Monica Bravin (pp.22,23); © René Caovilla (pp.28,29); © Museo della Calzatura Rossimoda (pp.32,33); © Louis Vuitton (pp.35,36,37); © Mavive (p.38); © Holly Snapp Gallery (p.52); © Boscolo Hotel dei Dogi (p.64); © Mia Nardi (p.65); © Hilton Molino Stucky (p.69); © Barovier & Toso (pp.82, 83); © Camilla Fabretti (pag. 85), © Chiara Pizzinato (p.87); © Fortuny SpA (pp.92-93); © Aperol (pp.108,109); © Paolo Spigariol, Nevio Doz (p.121); © Mattia Mionetto (pagg. 122-123), © Antonia Sautter Creations & Events (pp.124,125,126); © Caffè Florian (p.130); © Bogdanmocanu.ro (p.131); © Ca' Maria Adele (p.144); © Hotel Metropole (p.147); © O Jour (pp.150,151); © Silvia Zanella (p.155).

Printed and bound by
Conti Tipocolor – Calenzano (FI)

2015 © Gremese
New Books S.r.l. – Rome

All rights reserved. No part of this publication may be stored in a retrieval system, reproduced or transmitted, in any form or by any means, without the prior permission in writing of the Publisher.

ISBN 978-88-7301-774-5

Indice

Introduction 8
Venice and Its *Sestieri* 10

Fashion and Beauty

The *Papusse* of the Gondolier 12
I Need a Necklace 15
Curiosity – Impiraresse 16
Design Creations to Wear 18
Curiosity – The First Earrings… 21
My World in a Bag 23
Cameo – The Lady of the "R", Giuliana Coen a.k.a.
Roberta di Camerino 26
Shoes, Shoes, Shoes! 28
Curiosity – Venetian Ladies and High Heels ... 30
Shopping… at the Cinema! 34
Perfumes and Essences 38
Cameo – Isabella and Her "Secrets" 40
Curiosity – Venetian Blonde 42
A Loft Shop with a View of Gondolas 44
Pampering My Feet… in a Palace on the Grand Canal ... 46

Simple Pleasures

Printing Presses and Ink 48
Book Hunting 50
A Portrait Just for Me 53
In Casanova's Footsteps 54
Cameo – Sexy Venice: Veronica Franco and
the Venetian Courtesans 58
Curiosity – Tacàr botòn! (Chatting Up!) 60
Secret Gardens 62
To Touch the Sky with Your Fingertips 68

Get Dressed! We're Going Out! Music and Theater — 70
Curiosity – The Secret Message of the Bridge — 73
A Day of Meditation — 74
A "Liberty" *Aperitivo* — 76
Beauties on a Bike — 78
Murano… Reloaded — 82

Something for the House

"Velvet" Music — 86
Curiosity – Does Lace Come from Seaweed? — 88
The Witch's Mirror — 90
Fabrics… in an Ancient Monastery? — 92
Venice in Miniature — 94
Decoration Whims — 96
Cameo – The Last Dogaressa: Peggy Guggenheim — 100

Getting a Taste of Venice

Bàcari and *Ostarie* Hopping — 104
Curiosity – The Dogaressa's Fork — 107
Spritz!!! — 108
L'Antica Besseta — 111
The Bride's Coffee — 112
Chocotherapy! — 114
Impade, Haman's Ears and *Zuccherini*… — 116
Rings… to Eat? — 118
A Jewel to Sip — 120

Just Like a True Venetian

An Enchanted Evening: Carnival and the Doge's Ball — 124
Romantic Crusades: St. Mark's *Bocolo* — 128
Curiosity – "La biondina in gondoeta" (Boat Song) — 129
Marry Me in Venice! — 130
Cameo – A Queen in Venice? — 132

Fresco in a Gondola and *Costicine*	134
The "Famosissima" Night: *Il Redentore*	136
In Tintoretto's Studio	140
Cameo – Women Painters of the Serenissima	142
Seduce Me Tonight…	144
A Collection Hotel	146
Lose Yourself (and Find Yourself Again) in the Labyrinth of Love	148

"We Love Venice" (*from our Contributors*)

Giorgia Caovilla (Shoe Designer, "O Jour")	150
Manuela Pivato (Journalist, "Nuova Venezia")	152
Silvia Zanella (Caffè Florian Marketing Manager)	154
Holly Snapp (Owner and Manager of the Holly Snapp Gallery)	156

Introduction

"It is always assumed that Venice is the ideal place for a honeymoon. This is a grave error. To live in Venice or even to visit it, means that you fall in love with the city itself. There is nothing left over in your heart for anyone else..."

Peggy Guggenheim

Venice is a Lady.
This sophisticated *carnet d'adresses* was conceived by three Venetian women. Two of its authors were born in the city, the third "adopted" Venice heart and soul as her own. It celebrates the city that poet Gabriele D'Annunzio called "Anadyomene", or "Rising from the Sea". Indeed, just as Venus, Goddess of Beauty, Venice was born from the sea. We, the authors, hoped to share with our fellow "pretty" travelers – women who are always on the move and eager to explore just as we are – the excitement of living in Venice and visiting the city. The places we describe are dear to our hearts: they are the small chic boutiques we love, our favorite experiences

INTRODUCTION

and events, memories, the places where our friends work and create with such passion and talent. Page after page, Venice reveals herself to readers in a new, very special, and above all truly feminine light. This is also thanks to our four exceptional contributors who express their special bond with this city in such beautiful and moving words. The women highlighted in our historical "Cameos" are also unique. Whether endearing portraits of female artists, women of letters, courtesans or lacemakers, these cameos depict the feminine "weave" that has always been the rich fabric of life in Venice. This is our homage to these admirable and "glamorous" (before their time!☺) foremothers.

The "Treasure Hunt" hidden between the pages of this book is dedicated, on the other hand, to today's glamorous ladies: find the little Daisy and make your Venetian experience truly one of a kind! Or, should Venice still be just on your travel wish list, explore the Daisy-marked websites in the meantime, to already get a genuine touch of Venice.

My Pretty Venice is much more than a simple guide. It is a precious object of desire, a lovely gift for your girlfriends, the perfect book to pack for a weekend escape, or simply to leaf through to visit Venice... if only in your dreams!

Welcome to Venice!!

Isabella, Elisabeth and Beatrice

Venice and Its Sestieri

Venice is divided into six areas called *sestieri*. Historically, these were each represented by an advisor on the council of the doge, the chief magistrate and leader of the city. The elements of the *ferro da gondola*, or iron prow-head of a gondola, actually represent a curious and interesting stylized depiction of the city.
Venice's *sestieri* are:

Cannaregio: believed to be derived from *cannarecium*, which referred to the many rushes that grew in this marshy area at one time.

Castello: a reference to the medieval fortress around which the area developed.

Dorsoduro: literally "hard back", this suggests the extremely hard soil of the area that so differs from the clayish earth found generally.

San Marco: named after the Basilica dedicated to the city's patron saint.

San Polo: the central *sestiere* of the city, named after the church dedicated to Saint Paul, *Polo* in Venetian.

Santa Croce: the smallest *sestiere* of Venice, Santa Croce was also the name of a monastery that existed at one time.

VENICE AND ITS SESTIERI

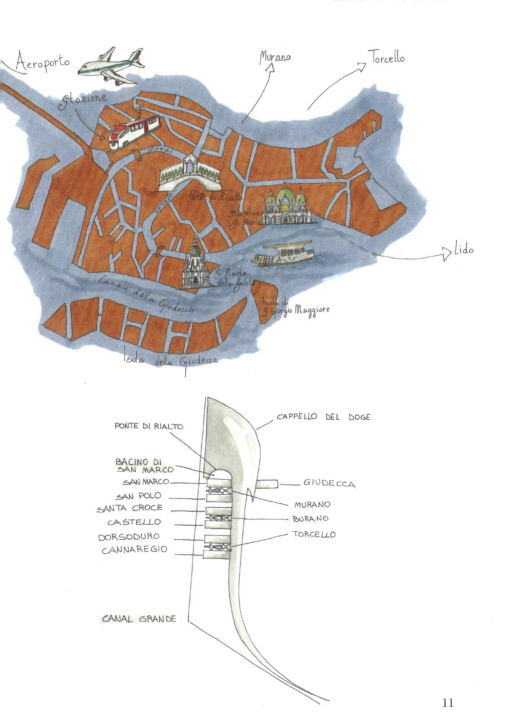

MY PRETTY VENICE

FASHION AND BEAUTY

The Papusse of the Gondolier

Here is a perfect example of chic recycling. The **"furlane"** (*papusse* in Venetian) are versatile velvet slippers that come in a rainbow of colors. They are worn by the most elegant ladies of the city to the most traditional gondoliers.

Though the slippers' vaguely Oriental-looking shape recalls the traditional Turkish variety, they were actually invented shortly after the end of WWII. At that time, they were made in the Friuli countryside using recyclable materials ranging from bicycle tires to scraps of cloth: often rather low-cut, the slippers were bound to the foot with an elastic band. This humble yet very practical type of footwear soon became all the rage in Venice too. The slippers were particularly popular with gondoliers, since their rubber soles did not damage the varnish of the gondolas and helped the gondoliers keep better balance while rowing.

Today, these slippers look just as good with a flowing caftan as with jeans, and are perfect for that casual *aperitivo* or as backup shoes after a night out dancing. Furlane, also made popular by Giorgio Armani, come in both the original version or as sabot. For truly personalized and original *furlane*, you can take or send your own fabric to the shop **Pied à Terre** (see below) that will create a custom-made pair just for you.

Pied à Terre
San Polo, Rialto 60
Tel. + 39 041 5285513
www.piedaterre-venice.com

FASHION AND BEAUTY

MY PRETTY VENICE

FASHION AND BEAUTY

I Need a Necklace

Under the frescoed vaulted ceilings of the Sotoportego degli Oresi, **Attombri**'s shop window transforms the ancient art of glass-bead jewelrymaking into an exciting contemporary expression.

Since 1987, Stefano and Daniele have been creating exclusive accessory-sculptures that boldly draw upon the traditional Venetian theme par excellence, glass, to interweave this element with silver, copper and a variety of other materials. All of the potential of ancient craftsmanship has been expanded by techniques invented by the two designers to produce objects today that are cherished, admired and distributed the world over. These works beautifully represent and promote the Venetian style, spreading its image across Europe, the United States, and even to Japan, where one-brand Attombri stores have been opened and a traveling "Attombri 20th Anniversary" exhibition was launched in 2007. Since its inception, Attombri has always been synonymous with prestigious names in the fashion industry. Dolce & Gabbana, Romeo Gigli and Pauly are only a few of the houses that have called upon the creations of the Venetian brothers. In addition to jewelry, the designers also create masterly crafted lights and décor objects.

Attombri
San Polo, Rialto 65
Tel. +39 041 5212524
www.attombri.com

Impiraresse

The dexterity of the *impiraresse* at work is both magical and poetic. Indeed, the *impiraresse* are famous for the fine art of threading tiny glass beads known as *conterie*, and work today just as they did centuries ago, with the same hypnotic agility and speed.
A *palmetta*, a "fan" of dozens of extremely thin needles, is plunged in the *sessola*, a small, curved wooden tray filled with the beads. The beads, as

they slide along the needle, are then gathered on pre-cut threads called "mazzette". Once threaded, the beads are ready to be used to create necklaces, flowers and elegant fringes.

In the past this ancient feminine craft was organized by intermediaries called *mistre*. They were the link between the *impiraresse*, who worked at home, and the bead factories. Crates of beads from the factory were delivered to the *mistre* who divided them into carefully weighed bags to be distributed to the *impiraresse*. The women would return the finished mazzette to them to receive payment for their work. The handicraft was widespread in Castello and Cannaregio, where the craftswomen were specialized in the creation of flowers for table decor or wedding bouquets, though it was also practiced on the Giudecca and, of course, in Murano, where the beads were actually made. The *impiraresse* were not very well paid, but their work did help to support the family. Often the *impiraresse* would work together, and especially in spring and summer, they formed chatty outdoor salons in front of their doors. There, they would exchange bits of gossip and also handy tips, such as how to pass the needle through their hair to make the threading process smoother.

Still today, the *impiraresse* tradition is kept alive by an annual "Festa delle *impiraresse*".

For info:
www.ferenaz.it/eventi.html.

Next to the railway station there is a workshop open to visitors. Though it produces necklaces for wholesalers, there are also documents and tools exhibited there, among the multicolored bags of beads. These objects tell the story of the impiraresse.

Ferenaz-Gioia di Luisa Conventi
Cannaregio, Calle Priuli 100
Tel. +39 041-5242822
www.ferenaz.it
By appointment only.

Design Creations to Wear

In the world of Murano glass, feminine creativity is expressed in a contemporary key by the sophisticated creations of two sisters, **Marina and Susanna Sent**. Their debut in the world of glass jewelry happened almost by sheer accident: after training in the family company, where they experimented in various processes and fusion techniques in decoration, polishing and sanding, they began to create bijoux that proved to be hugely popular just by word of mouth. Their creations, characterized by a rigorous formal purity that enhances the vivid fantasy of elements of color, were invited to be shown around the world: from the MoMAs of New York and Tokyo, to the Guggenheim Foundations of Venice and Bilbao. These were earrings, brooches and necklaces whose craftsmanship, through a process of simplification, evolved into bold design. And indeed, design, coupled with innovation and constant formal and technical experimentation, are the stylistic codes of the Sent sisters. Take the iconic collection "Soap", for example, that features clear glass bubbles threaded through a fishing line that seem to float suspended in the void, or the "Penelope" fabrics, made of beads with twin holes that inspired the creation of the magical dress christened "Debutto". Marina and Susanna's constant technical experimentation leads them to study an infinite variety of materials in their search for the most exciting combinations to marry with glass.

A visit to their Murano showroom is an experience not to be missed. It is a veritable "space to dream in", evoking the clean and impeccable lines of a museum of modern art. It is the perfect backdrop for their jewelry, fine objects and sculpture. These are all characterized by the innovative colors invented by the sisters, such as their deep purple and "ottanio" blue-green of the 1993 "Le Spezie" collection. Here are strong colors for strong and determined women: indeed, Marina and Susanna have passionately

FASHION AND BEAUTY

and enthusiastically sponsored the restoration of the fifteenth-century sculptures of Pierpaolo Dalle Masegne's "The Virtues" which are today housed in the Doge's Palace. The restoration project began with the statue "Fortitude". One of the sister's brooches was inspired by the shield of this statue, and thus became a brilliant example of how it is possible to rework suggestive elements of the distant past for today's creations.

Marina e Susanna Sent
Workshop and Showroom
Fondamenta Serenella, 20 (hours: Mon.-Fri. 10:00 am – 5:00 pm)
30141 Murano (VE)
Tel. +39 041 5274665
www.marinaesusannasent.com

The First Earrings…

… It would seem that earrings were worn for the first time in Venice in 1525: writer Marin Sanudo described a party at Palazzo Bragadin where one of his relatives "had her earlobes pierced as Moor women do, and she wore a thin gold ring with a large pearl dangling from it; something only she was wearing, and this rather displeased me".

FASHION AND BEAUTY

My World in a Bag

Three weeks. That is all **Monica Bravin** needs, with her agile and skilled fingers, to sew the hundreds of tiny, sparkling Swarowski crystals on the raffia knit of a deceptively simple bag, which is actually extremely sophisticated. Such are Monica's creations: each of them is a unique piece. Even when they might seem to be similar, there is always a detail that makes them different, perhaps the lining, the handle, a decorative bead, or a special button. Though Monica lets her flair and craftsmanship guide her, she draws inspiration directly from the materials she chooses with great care and painstaking attention. Her creations are also influenced by the close "collaboration" between Monica and her clients who, inevitably, also become her friends. We can find her exclusive bags at her shop in the heart of Rialto. In addition, in her constant search to meet new creative challenges, Monica has also recently launched a very original capsule collection of fabric-covered shoes. And, to appeal to a more British taste, there is an elegant selection of hand-crafted footwear for both men and women.

Style Shoes
San Polo, Ruga Rialto 409
Tel. +39 041 5228899

MY PRETTY VENICE

FASHION AND BEAUTY

Architectures in Fabric

The colored bands on the objects created by **Lauretta Vistosi** recall the works of Mondrian. Indeed, it is not surprising that one of her collections was dedicated to this Dutch painter. Lauretta's bags, diaries and other objects are characteristically decorated with brightly colored gros grain ribbons that stand out against a dark background: these are her "never-meeting" lines, and their colors are also found in the vivid *murrine* – some vintage, some contemporary – that decorate the objects.

These *murrine* are not only her characteristic signature, but are also the symbol of her heritage. Lauretta comes from a long line of venerable Murano glass-makers. In the sixties, the golden age of the Vistosi Glass Factory, she met designers Ettore Sottsass, Gae Aulenti and Angelo Mangiarotti. These artists and architects greatly influenced the style of her "architectures in fabric", such as the versatile "Ops Bags" and the eclectic "Vanity Birds", exquisite micro-bags that are so handy to carry your must-have items: lipstick and mobile phone!

Lauretta Vistosi
Dorsoduro,
Calle Lunga S. Barnaba 2866/B
Tel. +39 041 5286530
www.laurettavistosi.org

Cameo

The Lady of the "R", Giuliana Coen a.k.a. Roberta di Camerino

Like a well-kept secret, the charming Palazzo Loredan Grifalconi, where the Fondaco dei Curami once existed (where leather was worked during the Republic of Venice) is today home to the **Roberta di Camerino** atelier. This famous fashion house was founded by Giuliana Coen Camerino in 1945.

Giuliana has gone down in history for her extraordinary handbags, the first "*It Bags*", collected by fashion icons such as Princess Grace of Monaco, Joan Crawford, Farrah Fawcett, Isabella Rossellini and, more recently, by Madonna. These handbags, inspired by jewelry boxes just as well as doctors' bags, featured materials that were an intrinsic part of Venice's culture and history. The metal clasps and other details were fashioned by the same artisans who crafted the traditional decorations for gondolas. The designer used fabrics such as the sumptuous hand-woven silk velvets, then gave them a new original twist with happy-go-lucky bajadera stripes, *damier* patterns, *trompe-l'oeil* buckles and flaps and, of course, the ever-present initial "R".

The colors of these velvets were particularly captivating. Giuliana resolutely turned her back on the faded, dusty shades that were typical of Venetian fabrics of the time. She drew from the precious tones of the Renaissance: exuberant blues, reds and greens, the "colors of Tintoretto" as she loved to call them. She set these against a deep obsidian black and put them side by side with a new fuchsia pink, though often tempered by a chic beige, but also antagonized by vibrant orange or dense turquoise. The "textile illusions" Roberta di Camerino created for her famous jersey dresses were just as bold. These prints were sometimes composed of over twenty different shades or colors. Indeed, color, design and graphic experimentation were the essence of this revolutionary designer's style. The Roberta di Camerino atelier, whose suggestive atmosphere is heightened by an elegant collection of sculpted horses, also sells the latest creations of the label. It is also a chance to relive an absolutely extraordinary moment in the history of Italian fashion. Yet, there is also another place in Venice where the designer is still vividly present: the **Museo Storico Navale**, where a magnificent collection of seashells is tastefully exhibited. Giuliana donated this collection to the Museum to celebrate her everlasting love for the sea.

Roberta di Camerino
Palazzo Loredan Grifalconi
Cannaregio,
Calle della Testa 6359
Tel. +39 041 5237543
robertacamerino.tessa@gmail.com

**Museo Storico Navale
di Venezia**
Castello, Riva S. Biasio 2148
Tel. +39 041 2441399
www.marina.difesa.it/storiacultura/ufficiostorico/musei/museostoricove

Shoes, Shoes, Shoes!

In Venice a good pair of shoes is essential. A visit to the city will mean being on your feet all day, every day, and everyone will definitely notice your footwear. So, beautiful yet comfortable shoes are a must!

The custom-made shoes that **Giovanna Zanella** designs for both men and women in her studio not far from Rialto are exciting. The inspiration for her whimsical creations, she says, comes from living life with her eyes wide open and, thanks to her artisan skills, she infuses this ancient craft with an original contemporary *esprit*. This is expressed through an intriguing choice of leathers in the most vibrant colors, that are then combined with nylon sprays, fringes, flowers and appliqués. Certainly just what you need to lighten your step on the "masegni", those (in)famous grey stones of the calli!

Not only for a magical evening, but also for everyday elegance, perfection awaits in the "Dream Called Shoe" creations by **René Caovilla**. Elegant

décolleté with vertiginous high heels, sensuous hand-made sandals richly decorated with crystals and lace, boots in precious skins and leathers, not to mention lines of flats and ballerinas that all stylishly exalt yet hug the shape of our feet. The symbol of this fashion brand is the mythical "Snake" sandal, launched in 1975, and today the griffe's official logo. It was an ancient gold snake-shaped bracelet in the Naples Museum of Archeology that inspired this sophisticated creation that winds around the ankle with a precious string of crystals. Exhibited at the MoMA in New York, it has been revisited in countless variations and themes, decorated with beads, paillettes, strass and stones, to create patterns of butterflies, shells and flowers in multicolored tones or solids – the ideal shoe for dancing on the exquisite ballroom floors of a Venetian palace!

Yet when your precious shoes cry out for some special care, it's time for **Serafino**. Talented Aldo has been skillfully "restoring" and proudly highlighting quality footwear in his tiny workshop for over 50 years. And his craft does not end there: his clients come from all the world knowing that he can perfectly reproduce a favorite pair of shoes, or "rejuvenate" the look of any beloved, yet perhaps rather dated, footwear!

Giovanna Zanella
Castello, San Lio 5641
Tel. +39 041 5235500
www.giovannazanella.it

René Caovilla
San Marco, Salizada San Moisé 1296
Tel. +39 041 5238038
www.renecaovilla.com

Serafino il Calzolaio
San Polo, Rio Terà San Silvestro 1058/A
Cell. +39 338 4308906

Venetian Ladies and High Heels

Venetian ladies have always loved their high heels. During the Renaissance they proudly showed off their impossible "calcagnetti", a type of footwear "perched" on a wedge that could be a half a meter high. Then it was absolutely necessary for aristocratic ladies to be accompanied by no less than two servants during their (usually brief!!!) outings.

The city's Senate finally forbade the use of these shoes since the frequent falls from these "altitudes" often caused injuries or even miscarriages. Nevertheless, *calcagnetti* continued to be worn until they slowly went out of fashion. Artisan shoemakers and cobblers formed a guild of "*calegheri*", whose Gothic headquarters is still visible on Campo San Tomà. In the lunette over the door, a 1478 relief depicts St. Mark healing cobbler Anianus, who became the patron saint of shoemakers. Some representations of coeval footwear decorate the lintel. For centuries, and most particularly during the capricious eighteenth century, the *calegheri* created veritable masterpieces for the little feet of chic Venetian women: elegant embroidered leather sabots, flirty mules made in silk damasks, and shoes made to match the fabric of a dress, or decorated with shiny silver buckles …

Today's Venetian women are no less glamorous and, though they continue to wear their heels with great panache, they are somewhat wiser. Since all Venetians walk at least a couple of hours a day, ladies often have a "spare" pair of shoes with them. It is not uncommon to arrive at a party and see

the same ladies who had been flying over the calli in comfortable flats or *furlane*, nonchalantly slipping into ethereal high heels that will again be changed for the walk back home.

For shoe lovers (and who isn't???), a visit to the **Shoe Museum Rossimoda** is truly a must. Housed in the magnificent Villa Foscarini Rossi on the Brenta Riviera, just a short drive out of Venice, visitors discover a historical collection of eighteenth and nineteenth-century footwear, as well as over 1700 pairs of shoes produced by Rossimoda from 1947 to the present day.

Museo della calzatura Rossimoda
Villa Foscarini Rossi
Via Doge Pisani 1/2 – 30039 Stra (VE)
Tel. +39 049 9801091
www.museodellacalzatura.it

And absolutely not to be missed is the **outlet shopping** in the area. This quarter, famous since the seventeenth century for the production of footwear, is where the shoes of such brands as Jimmy Choo, Marc Jacobs, Donna Karan and Celine are produced, just to name a few.
Definitely worth a visit are:

Voltan, 1898
Via Venezia 121 – 30039 Stra (VE) – Tel. +39 049 502233

Henderson Outlet Calzature
Via Padova 214 – 30030 Tombelle di Vigonovo (VE) – Tel. +39 049 502652

Calzaturificio Ballin
Vic. B. Cellini 4 – 30032 Fiesso d'Artico (VE) – Tel. +39 041 5137211

Shopping... at the Cinema!

The Mostra Internazionale d'Arte Cinematografica was created in 1932. The Lido was in fact the hub of the event, with its glamorous beaches and luxury hotels. Then, a few years later, to give the seventh art a focal point in the center of the city too, a 'Fenice of cinema' was inaugurated: the Cinema San Marco, designed by architect Brenno Del Giudice. The rationalist design of his project, characterized by a very essential yet dynamic style, was a balance between the Venetian architectural tradition and a contemporary approach. Though the wide cantilevered balcony was reminiscent of naval architecture, the reliefs created by Napoleone Martinuzzi and the mosaics by Guido Cadorin paid tribute to the great Venetian artistic heritage.

The revolutionary building is today the Venetian headquarters of the Maison **Louis Vuitton**. Through the metamorphosis from movie theater to luxury store, the edifice has preserved the elegant and understated essence of the original structure. Here, the world of Vuitton dedicated to men, women, and travel, becomes a flowing crescendo of shopping temptations on every floor. The story of the intense bond between the Maison Vuitton and Venice is also told through strategically placed works of art by Candida Höfer, Jean-François Rauzier and Humberto & Fernando Campana. They suggest a daring and creative new concept of the city. The Campana brothers' work "Fragments" is fascinating. It assembles the famous Venini "handkerchiefs" in a luminous sculpture installation that highlights the techniques used to create Murano glass. Last but not least, on the top floor, a gem awaits connoisseurs: the Espace Culturel and its sophisticated bookshop, a goldmine of volumes on history, art and lifestyle "alla veneziana". The elegant temporary exhibitions also shown there create infinite innovative possibilities to lovers of Venice thanks to the Maison's official partnership with the Fondazione Musei Civici di Venezia. This space, conceived as a dialogue between past and present, reflects Louis Vuitton's philosophy: to preserve, share, and continue to nurture an ever-evolving cultural heritage.

FASHION AND BEAUTY

Louis Vuitton Venice Maison
San Marco, Salizada San Moisè 1345
Tel. +39 041 8844318
www.louisvuitton.com

P.S. The mosaics once present in the foyer of the Cinema San Marco may now be found in the hall of the nearby Hotel Monaco & Grand Canal. There, you can follow in Casanova's footsteps ... but that's another story! (See pp. 54-55)

MY PRETTY VENICE

FASHION AND BEAUTY

– MY PRETTY VENICE –

Perfumes and Essences

To enter the spezieria on Campo San Fantin is to step back in time: from the mid-seventeenth century this space, in the heart of the city, was home to an ancient *spezieria* (apothecary) dedicated to Saint Paul. In 1846, the architect Giambattista Meduna, creator of the Gran Teatro La Fenice that overlooks this same *campo*, redesigned its interiors. He created a precious alluring space that today has been returned to its original splendor through an impressively faithful restoration project. The four statues by Pietro Zandomeneghi, that embody Botany, Medicine, Surgery and Physics, powerfully grace the space surrounded by twelve smaller allegorical figures. The central counter, in rich walnut, is decorated by a relief depicting the alembics of an alchemist's laboratory. The entire atmosphere perfectly re-creates the life of an ancient apothecary, a place where Venetians would go not only to buy remedies, unguents and perfumes, but also to meet and exchange news and gossip. And, it is in the wake of this great Venetian perfume heritage, that the company Mavive, creator of "The Merchant of Venice" line, embarked on this exciting adventure, undertaking the restoration of this prestigious

FASHION AND BEAUTY

space. Here, the flagship store of its high-end perfumery line of the same name, has found a home. The line offers fragrances and objects that reflect the ancient Venetian art of perfumery. They are inspired by the "mude", the naval convoys that traveled from Venice to faraway Oriental ports for exotic spices and essences to bring back to the lagoon. In addition to the line's forty *eaux de toilette* with their elegant bottles in bright Venetian red, there is a collection in prestigious Murano glass. Anyone who desires a completely customized essence may even mix her own fragrances with the exclusive "Perfume Kit".

To further discover the fascinating world of perfume, Mavive, in collaboration with the Fondazione Musei Civici di Venezia, designed and sponsored a fascinating educational-olfactory experience. This may be explored at the Palazzo Mocenigo museum where, in addition to rooms devoted to the history of fashion and textiles, visitors will find exhibits on the history and production of fragrances.

Flagship store
San Marco, Campo San Fantin 1895
Tel. +39 041 296 0559
www.themerchantofvenice.it

Museo di Palazzo Mocenigo
Santa Croce, Salizada San Stae 1992
Tel. +39 041 721798
http://mocenigo.visitmuve.it

Isabella and Her "Secrets"

Venice has always been renowned for the attractiveness of her women, a beauty that was often achieved by the use of "secret" beauty products. These were made at home in the early days, but were later skillfully mixed by expert chemists-cum-herbalists known as *spezieri*. In 1561 these precious beauty secrets were published by Isabella Cortese in a book with the exhaustive title *I secreti della signora Isabella Cortese né quali si contengono cose minerali, medicinali, arteficiose e alchimiche, e molte de l'arte profumatoria, appartenenti a ogni gran Signora* ("The secrets of Signora Isabella Cortese containing things mineral, medicinal, artificial and alchemical, and many from the art of perfumery, belonging to any fine Lady").

In this book, admired and read by women all over Europe, Isabella, an alchemist and a writer (although some historians claim that "Isabella" was the pseudonym for Timoteo Rossello), describes recipes for dyes and inks, though more importantly, also beauty powders, soaps and scented waters. These were made from the exotic ingredients that regularly arrived in the city from the East.

Among the most curious recipes: a facial cream made with a mixture of rose water, cinnamon, rock salt and the "urine of a virgin boy"; or an extremely dangerous depilatory cream made of quicklime. There are also the how-to instructions for the so-called "pezzuole di Levante". These were small scraps of fabric soaked in a mixture of rock alum, quicklime and *verzino*, a dye from the plant *Caesalpinia brasiliensis*, more commonly known in Europe as "Brasil" and from which a vivid red dye was obtained. The *pezzuole* were used to color the cheeks or as lip rouge, but Venetian courtesans used them to also color their nipples, making them more… inviting!!

Venetian Blonde

Let's clarify: this is not real blonde. The color generally defined as "Venetian blonde" is actually a shade enriched by deep, warm red undertones, magnificently expressed by the great artists of the Serenissima, Jacopo Tintoretto, Paolo Veronese and, of course, Titian. Indeed, it is no wonder that this color is also known as "Titian Red". Considered a symbol of purity and innocence, a lavish blonde mane was the ardent desire of any Venetian woman. Above all, brides-to-be. They would enrich the highlights in their hair by blending thin, long gold threads into their bridal coiffure.

To achieve the desired shade, however, it was necessary to undergo a tedious (and rather stinky too! ☺) process. This began by mixing "bionda", a homemade dye mixture of some very unusual ingredients: among these, turmeric, saffron, rock alum, lemon juice, white wine, Arabic gum, dried Centaurea petals, ammonia and urine.

Once the dye had been distilled, Venetian ladies went up to their *altane*, the typical terraces perched above many of the roofs of Venice. Dressed in a light linen or silk tunic called *schiavoneto*, they would cover their heads with a *solana*, a straw hat with a cut-out crown. They would spread the locks of their hair over the brim of the hat and, using a little sponge, the *sponzeta*, they kept their hair constantly soaked with the "*bionda*". The combined action of the bionda and the rays of the sun guaranteed hair fit for a portrait!

A very special address to try the mythical Venetian red?

Hair by Design
Michele Doardo
Cannaregio, Salizada del Pistor 4552
Tel. +39 041 5287217

A Loft Shop with a View of Gondolas

A refined and minimal space: **Ottico Fabbricatore**. This is one of the oldest and most well-known optical shops of Venice, and has always been loved for its extraordinary eyeglasses in the most original forms, exclusive designs, and the use of rare materials ranging from American buffalo horn, worked in Germany, to ultimate lightweight titanium. Thanks to owner Francesco Lincetto's highly creative wife Marianna, in recent years Ottico Fabbricatore is not only the best place for designer eyewear: the couple's shop window now already lures you in with beautiful handbags designed by Marianna herself. Her creations, admired for their pure essential lines and quality craftsmanship, are available in a myriad of colors and hides, and even to order.

Recently the historic shop has opened up a new space: across a quaint courtyard, we are led to the highly eclectic design proposed by L'O.FT. This is a true concept store where vintage furniture serves as the backdrop for sophisticated Made-In-Italy collections, exclusive productions, lingerie lines, body creams and accessories for the home. Though Francesco and Marianna also plan to open up L'O.FT's evocative atmosphere to exhibitions and events, customers can already enjoy the view of passing gondolas from the adorable little salotto that overlooks a canal just a few steps from the Grand Canal and Rialto: a truly Venetian, and absolutely glamorous, break!

Ottico Fabbricatore
San Marco, Calle del Lovo 4773
Cell. +39 393 3359709

FASHION AND BEAUTY

Pampering My Feet...
in a Palace on the
Grand Canal

After a long day exploring Venice, what could be more welcome than some special treatment for our feet, perhaps in a chic spa set in a Renaissance palace?

Palazzo Papadopoli is one of the most imposing buildings overlooking the Grand Canal. Built near Rialto by the Coccina family in the sixteenth century, it later became home to the aristocratic Tiepolos. The family enriched its interior with extraordinary frescoes and an extraordinary library. In 1864 the Palazzo was acquired by the Papadopoli counts who began an ambitious restoration project which included the creation of two gardens. Since 2013, the stunning Palazzo is home to the **Aman Canal Grande Venice**, a hotel which is one of the pride and joys of the owners of Aman Resorts.

Soft lighting, intimate spaces, and the intoxicating scents of essential oils: the spa of the Hotel is a veritable sanctuary of well-being, for the body and the spirit. Located in an extremely private space on the third floor of the Palazzo, it proposes a splendid menu of rituals for face and body. The "Signature Foot Treatment" is quintessential pampering for the feet: it offers a Himalayan salt scrub to balance the circulatory system, a mint and Arnica massage to calm the feet, and a hot compress to relax them. To complete the treatment, you can choose to have a head or hand massage too.

After all of this pampering, take a moment to visit a little curiosity. Go to the second floor of the Palazzo and find the "Sala del Piedino", the "Little Foot Room". There, a little stucco foot peeks out from a very ancient fresco! Finally, after a romantic tea served in the ballroom, or a drink in

FASHION AND BEAUTY

the garden, you will feel truly refreshed and pampered... from head... to toe!!!

To book:

Aman Canal Grande Venice Spa
Palazzo Papadopoli
San Polo, Calle Tiepolo 1364
Tel. +39 041 2707750
amancanalgrandevenice.spa@amanresorts.com

SIMPLE PLEASURES

Printing Presses and Ink

In the city made famous by Aldus Manutius' typographic genius, we are not surprised to find the noble art of printing still very much alive in the workshop of **Gianni Basso**, created in 1984. Here, just as during the Renaissance, father and son work side by side among manual printing presses and the scent of ink.

Do as celebrities such as Hugh Grant or Ben Affleck (yet the list is endless!!) do. Come to this tiny printing shop on the Calle del Fumo and order unique and exclusive business cards embellished with one of the hundreds of ancient Venetian motifs, styles ranging from Renaissance to Gothic, Byzantine, and more! Basso also creates prints of Venice and sophisticated bookmarks, bookplates and elegant stationery that can be shipped directly home: the addresses from customers from every part of the world that line his counters are a testimony to Basso's tremendous international appeal. His engravings of Venice or elegant bookmarkers make perfect gifts too.

A visit here is a plunge back into the history of printing: this is a veritable passion for Gianni, and he is always eager to talk about every aspect of the craft. He will also tell you some of the stories of the ancient motifs and decorations – a fascinating conversation!

Tipografia Gianni Basso
Cannaregio, Calle del Fumo 5306
Tel. +39 041 5234681

SIMPLE PLEASURES

Book Hunting

Venice was where the first Koran in Arabic was published, and the earliest writings on alchemy or cuisine were printed. To set out on a rare book expedition seems almost a duty, and original bookshops, just as libraries, abound in the city.

For example, a truly unique experience awaits visitors at the bookstore **Acqua Alta**. Brimming with new and used books in all languages, the focus is mainly on the city of Venice, though we can also find delightful old comic books and magazines, art books, novels, and … the owner's kitties tiptoeing about the old book-filled canoes, bathtubs, and even a real gondola that sits right in the middle of the main room. The staircase is a real surprise: it is actually made from old encyclopedia volumes. There is a wonderful view from the upper level of the Canal and the "Corte Sconta" straight out of Corto Maltese's adventures.

The **Libreria Bertoni** is another goldmine for book lovers. Founded in 1935, it has been run by three generations of booksellers and is specialized in out-of-print works. The bookshop's tantalizing choice of topics ranges from art, architecture, photography, Venetian culture and history, all available with attractive discounts. And, with a little luck and patience, you might even find that wonderful catalogue of the exhibition you never got to see …

Libreria Acqua Alta
Castello, Calle Lunga Santa Maria Formosa 5176/B
Tel. +39 041 2960841

Libreria Bertoni Venezia
San Marco, Calle de la Mandola 3637/B
Tel. +39 041 5229583
www.bertonilibri.com

Among Venice's many impressive libraries, the **Fondazione Querini Stampalia** is truly one of a kind: its collections offer not only a section devoted to Venice, but also include books on law and economics, literature and art. Another interesting feature? According to the founder's express wishes, the Library remains open even in the evenings and on holidays. Not to be missed is also a peek inside the Fondazione's **Q-shop** where craftsmen present their original handcrafted objects and works to the general public. The shop's selection of books is also unique, with a large section devoted to children, as well as fine volumes on architecture, design, and guides on ancient and modern art.

Biblioteca Querini Stampalia and Q-shop
Fondazione Querini Stampalia ONLUS
Castello, Campo Santa Maria Formosa 5252
Tel. +39 041 2711411
www.querinistampalia.org

MY PRETTY VENICE

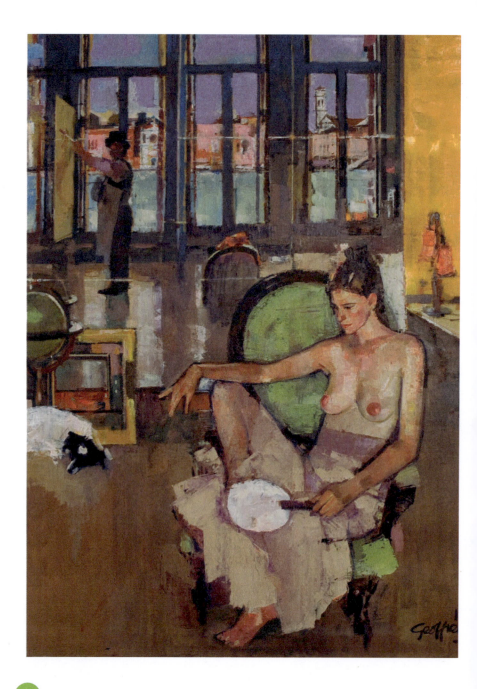

A Portrait Just for Me

There is a studio with a magnificent view over the Canale della Giudecca where "opium divans" and silver candelabras, sumptuous silks and Oriental parasols, fans and painter's palettes fill a bright space enveloped by the voluptuous melodies of jazz and blues. This is the perfect backdrop for artist **Geoffrey Humphries'** sensuous and elegant figures.

One of the most important figurative painters living in Venice, Geoffrey Humphries was born in England and moved to Venice in 1966, where he graduated from the Accademia di Belle Arti di Venezia (1974). His works are admired the world over: his watercolors that explore the secret corners of Venice, but above all, his audacious ladies slipping off their nonchalantly untied kimonos, or his nude studies that have been acquired by many European and American private collectors, while other works have been exhibited at the National Portrait Gallery and Royal Portrait Society in London.

Let yourself be seduced by the tradition of beautiful women in Venetian painting made famous by Palma il Vecchio, Titian and Tintoretto. Why not treat yourself to a sensuous, slightly boudoir painting of yourself for the bedroom? This little luxury is surprisingly accessible: a small oil painting, that would only take an afternoon of posing, would start from 2,000 Euros.

Holly Snapp Gallery
San Marco, Calle delle Botteghe 3133
Tel. +39 041 2960824
www.hollysnappgallery.com

In Casanova's Footsteps

The presence of the world's most illustrious womanizer, Giacomo Casanova, can still be strongly felt in his native city of Venice: palaces, *casini*, monasteries, and even *bàcari* all preserve the memory of his passage. Casanova recounted his legendary amorous adventures in his *Memoires*. They trace an evocative itinerary that we can follow through Venice's libertine eighteenth century. This begins with the house where his mother and sister lived, the **Palazzo Merati alle Fondamente Nove**, with its sumptuous interior that still preserves its elegant alcove decorated in gilt stucco.

At the **Do Spade**, in Rialto, Casanova often drank *ombre* and ate *cicheti*. His friend Giorgio Baffo, a famous local erotic poet who initiated Giacomo to the art of love, lived on Campo San Maurizio. After Casanova's sacrilegious and intense romantic relationship with the (never explictly) identified nun M.M. of the **Santa Maria degli Angeli** monastery in Murano, the ardent young man was condemned to five years imprisonment at Piombi, a wretched prison in the **Palazzo Ducale**, accessible from the Bridge of Sighs. It was only after some plotting and athletic prowess, that he was able to flee from the prison after only fifteen months. According to legend, before escaping to the mainland, Casanova indulged in the luxury of a coffee on St. Marks' square, perhaps at the legendary **Caffè Florian**. He had often slipped away for romantic encounters in the gardens of the Giudecca, the same gardens that are today the grounds of the luxury Belmond Hotel Cipriani. This is the favorite of many Hollywood stars (George Clooney is a regular here!). The manicured **Giardino Casanova** delights visitors with its verdant pergolas, pomegranate trees, azaleas, and the scent of roses and lavender. After this total immersion in green, perhaps an aperitivo by the pool, followed by dinner with an unforgettable view of St. Mark's?

If there is one place in particular that evokes the decadent and unbridled spirit of Casanova's Venice, it is in the precious interiors of the **Ridotto** in the Palazzo Dandolo, now part of the Hotel Monaco & Grand Canal.

These elegant spaces, enriched by magnificent stucco decoration, were often the favorite haunts of Giacomo and many noblemen and ladies. Here they whiled away the hours gambling and weaving their secret liaisons, their identities hidden by the *baute* and *morette* masks. At times, losses at the gambling table were so disastrous, or a meeting so secret, that the use of a discreet – and still today existent – side exit (that led directly to the canal and an awaiting gondola) obliged.

And, if you surrender to the luxury of one of the extraordinary New Years or Carnival parties organized by the Hotel Monaco & Grand Canal, you will feel all of the excitement of an evening spent with Casanova!

Palazzo Merati alle Fondamente Nove
Cannaregio, Corte Berlendis 6293
www.valorizzazioniculturali.com/palazzo-merati

Cantina Do Spade
San Polo, Calle de le Do Spade 859
Tel. +39 041 5210583
www.cantinadospade.com

Targa Casa Baffo
Campo San Maurizio

Chiesa di Santa Maria degli Angeli
Murano, ACTV Lines 4.1 and 4.2, Venier stop.

Piombi, Palazzo Ducale
http://palazzoducale.visitmuve.it/it/il-museo/percorsi-e-collezioni/itinerari-segreti/

MY PRETTY VENICE

Caffè Florian
Piazza San Marco
Tel. +39 041 5205641
www.caffeflorian.com

Hotel Monaco & Grand Canal
San Marco, Calle Vallaresso 1332
Tel. +39 041 5200211
www.hotelmonaco.it

Belmond Hotel Cipriani
Giudecca,
Fondamenta
San Giovanni 10
Tel. +39 041 5207744
www.belmond.com/it/hotel-cipriani-venice
The Hotel and gardens are open from March to October.

Sexy Venice: Veronica Franco and the Venetian Courtesans

In 1509 there were no fewer than 11,164 prostitutes in Venice. "Love for sale" was easy to find, especially in the Castelletto, an area between Rialto and San Polo characterized by just one way in and out. These "ladies" worked in houses managed by a madam who kept the accounts and duly paid their income taxes. The "carampane" as they were known, since most of the ladies lived in houses owned by the Rampani family ("ca" meaning "street"), would customarily appear enticingly half-nude at their windows – no wonder there is a bridge nearby called the "Ponte delle Tette" ("Tits Bridge"!)… When making their rounds about the city in search of customers, prostitutes were made to wear a yellow veil as a distinguishing sign, and at the third toll of St. Mark's bells, they were to return to their quarters. Courtesans, on the other hand, enjoyed a totally different social status. Well-educated, elegant, highly trained in the arts of music, singing, and brilliant conversation, these fascinating escorts received their guests in sumptuous boudoirs. These were extravagant chambers with alluring frescoed ceilings, walls adorned with gilt leather, silk drapes, and

mirrors. A courtesan's luxury wardrobe was studied to highlight her sensuality, with audacious "drawers" beneath her skirt, and high heels. Courtesans were forbidden by law to wear pearls, a symbol of Venice's aristocratic married ladies, so they wore necklaces of glass beads instead. Nevertheless, courtesans would often flauntingly wear beautiful fine silks, though this was also against the law. They enjoyed prestige and social standing and, bedecked in furs and jewels, were habituées of the best literary and artistic salons. The Renaissance writer, poet and playwright Pietro Aretino, in an invitation to Titian in December 1547, promised "A couple of pheasants and I'm not sure what else await you for dinner, along with Miss Angiola Zaffetta!" Often the courtesans' favors were used as means to "diplomatic" ends. In the summer of that same 1547, Venice welcomed Henry II of France. Among the pleasures offered to the king was a night with the famous courtesan Veronica Franco, who was also a writer and a poet. In her later years, driven by her desire to redeem herself, Veronica bequeathed funds for the creation of the Casa del Soccorso, a charitable institution dedicated to "repentant" courtesans and prostitutes.

A lunch or dinner inspired by this theme? The Trattoria **Antiche Carampane** is in Venice's ancient red light district. A sign on the door warns, "No Pizza, No Lasagna, No Tourist Menu". This is the place for fresh fish and genuine Venetian cuisine…

Trattoria Antiche Carampane
San Polo, Rio Terà Rampani 1911
Tel. +39 041 5240165
www.antichecarampane.com

Tacàr botòn! (Chatting Up!)

The charming femininity of Venetian women has always taken advantage of some precious allies in the game of seduction: in the eighteenth century, women used their fans to transmit coded messages to their suitors; in the nineteenth, the shawl became the favorite "tool" of these fascinating enchantresses. Long shawls in silk or wool have been made in Venice since at least 1761, as documented by the license dated that year granted to Giovanni Zivaglio to "produce kerchiefs as they use in India and are worn by the women of the Kingdom of the Persian Shah". Thus, they were christened "shawls" and were worn by the women of the people, but also by bourgeois ladies. These shawls were descendents of the *zendali*, the *nizioleti* and the *fazuoli*, large squares of cloth that women of the Serenissima had always used to cover their heads and shoulders. The new version, however, was now trimmed around the edges with very long fringe, and often embroidered. Originally shawls were worn in a variety of colors. In 1848, however, in sign of mourning for the soldiers fallen during the War of Independence, they appeared only in sober black. Worn with style and brio, the shawl, "with its deep artistic folds that caress a woman's curves and give an alluring gracefulness and unparalleled softness to the female body, enriching it with a mysterious charm..." (E.M. Baroni, *Lo scialle veneziano*, 1921) was slipped from the shoulders with studied nonchalance, or draped in countless ways that were christened with such creative names as "Carmen's", "sailor's" or "nun's" style.
The fringe trimming around these shawls was used to play a naughty trick: when a woman walked past her sweetheart, she made the fringe swing in such a way that, almost by chance, it got caught on the buttons of the man's jacket: hence the saying "Tacar boton" (literally "to stitch on a button").

You can buy a Venetian shawl at:

Sartoria dei Dogi
Santa Croce, Calle del Tentor 1840-1842
Tel. +39 041 713838
www.sartoriadeidogi.it

"Co se slonga la franza, se scurta la virtù.
E le pute de un tempo non le se trova più."
(*"The longer the fringe, the shorter is virtue.
And the girls that were, may be found no more."*)

MY PRETTY VENICE

Secret Gardens

"[...] you need to look for them between the inextricable squiggles of the city, in the most remote places..."
Henri de Régnier, *Esquisses vénitiennes* (Paris, 1910, p. 10)

Veritable Venetian paradises may often be glimpsed simply by peeking through a wrought iron gate. Palazzo gardens, convent vegetable plots, private courtyards richly decorated with sculptures, pergolas, *vere da pozzo* (well heads), flower beds and rose gardens, all create a miraculous green mosaic throughout the city. These Gardens of Eden, almost invariably hidden behind venerable walls, have been proudly maintained by the Venetians for centuries. With patience and tenacity, the people have managed to save them from the high tide of the lagoon waters.

Cà Zenobio Garden

In the eighteenth century this elegant space was lined with a very elaborate formal *parterre*, though during the following century, it was transformed into a romantic garden. The Garden belongs to the Baroque palace of the same name owned by the Armenian Mekhitarist Congregation. From the gate, the vanishing point of the panorama leads to the neoclassical "Casin", built by Tommaso Temanza in 1777. Little walkways, hillrocks, and an unusual suspension bridge date back to the nineteenth century.

Dorsoduro, Fondamenta del Soccorso 2596
www.mekhitar.com

Fondazione Querini Stampalia Garden

This contemporary garden designed by Carlo Scarpa takes a new look at the Venetian tradition, enriching it with Arab and Japanese influences.

The lawn's simplicity is punctuated by a careful selection of trees chosen for their size and flowering time, and by a tiered pool in copper, cement and mosaic which in turn flows into a little canal that ends in a flourish on both sides by marble stones decorated with a maze pattern. A Gothic lion and an ancient well head recall the strong ties with the history of the city.

Castello, Campo Santa Maria Formosa 5252
Tel. +39 041 2711411
www.querinistampalia.org

An Artist's Garden in Murano: The Honey Garden

This garden was created in the spring of 2013 by artist Judi Harvest on the occasion of her exhibition "Denatured: Honeybees + Murano". She wished to create a home for a new colony of bees, since honeybees have been the main source of inspiration for her work for years. Set in an unused field beside, and that still belongs, to the artistic glass factory "Linea Arianna", where the artists' glassworks are actually made, the garden is a mixture of sweet-smelling pomegranate, pear and apple trees and thick lavender and sage bushes. Definitely the main attraction of the garden are the multicolored beehives from which the bees travel for foraging pollen for a 3 mile-radius every day: the dense honey they produce has the scent of beautiful purple Barena flowers from the Venice lagoon as the dominant flavor.

Vetreria artistica Linea Arianna
Località Sacca Serenella, Murano
By appointment only.
Tel. +39 041 736619
http://judiharvest.net/

You can see the garden on Facebook:
https://facebook.com/honeygardenmurano

An Echo Game

The quiet secret garden of Palazzo Rizzo-Patarol, today the luxury Grand Hotel dei Dogi, is not only a place to relax, have a drink, or enjoy a good book. There is also an amazing curiosity hidden here. Beneath a small artificial hillrock you will find a curious little *grotin del giasso* (an artificial cave made of brick where blocks of ice were once stored to preserve food). Peek inside and ask a question: thanks to the astounding acoustics, your echo will come back with the answer!

Boscolo Hotel dei Dogi
Cannaregio, Fondamenta della Madonna dell'Orto 3499
Tel. +39 041 2208111   *http://venezia.boscolohotels.com/contatti/*

SIMPLE PLEASURES

Villa Groggia Park

This romantic eighteenth-century park, embellished with small hillrocks, classical "ruins", walkways and great stones, is today a favorite spot among Venetian youngsters to stage their intrepid adventures, though there are also shady corners that offer quiet spaces to study, meditate, or simply catch your breath. There is also a lovely surprise: on the spot where a shooting gallery once stood, visitors discover a little theater built with recycled materials from nearby palaces.

Wearable Gardens

Precious tulips with sapphire pistils hidden in their corollas, brightly colored daisies and roses made of enamel and precious stones: these are the trademarks of the imaginary "Wearable Gardens" of rings, earrings and necklaces in the new Mia Nardi collection. Then, the memory of idyllic Venetian gardens will always be with you…

Nardi Venezia
Piazza San Marco 71/A
Tel. +39 041 5225733
www.mianardi.com

MY PRETTY VENICE

To Touch the Sky with Your Fingertips

Exploring the Venetian *calli* is a magical adventure. Yet to experience the superb view of the city from atop its extraordinary architectural creations, that often on a clear morning are framed by the majestic Dolomites in the distance, is truly unforgettable.

The bell tower of St. Mark's Basilica for this treat usually comes to mind, but the queues for the visit are often daunting. So, here's a tip: the panorama from the **bell tower of San Giorgio Maggiore**, just facing St. Mark's, is just as enchanting and definitely less crowded. Dating back to 1467, the bell tower collapsed in 1774 to then be rebuilt by Benedetto Buratti in 1791. The structure's height of 75 meters makes it one of the tallest bell towers in the city, and its belfry is easily accessible by elevator. In an almost secret corner of the north lagoon, an extraordinary soaring view is offered by the eleventh-century **Torcello bell tower**: from the jade-colored waters, magical islands emerge, while at your feet the Byzantine Venetian gem, the Basilica of Santa Maria Assunta with its magnificent mosaics, appears. A visit to this island, inhabited by only fourteen souls, will also be the chance to discover curiosities such as its suggestive "Devil's Bridge", a rare example of an ancient bridge without any side posts; the so-called "Attila's Throne", a marble throne seat probably belonging to the bishop of Torcello, and the famous "Locanda Cipriani", Hemingway's favorite hangout, and where he authored *Across the River and into the Trees*.

You can also enjoy quite a fascinating view, although perhaps in a less mystical or literary mood, from the terrace of the **Skyline Rooftop Bar** of the Hilton Molino Stucky Hotel on the Giudecca. An ideal location for romantic evenings, private events and exclusive parties during Carnival, Il Redentore, or the Venice Film Festival, its famous pool parties palpitate to the exhilarating beats of the DJs. In the summer, the Skylunch Restaurant offers a unique selection of *tartares* and innovative fusion cuisine.

Finally, to truly touch the sky with your fingertips, the bravest visitors can experience the excitement of actually flying over the lagoon: try **Volavenezia** and its customized tours.

Campanile di San Giorgio
Isola San Giorgio Maggiore
Tel. +39 041 5227827 (Call to check opening times)

Campanile della basilica di Torcello
Isola di Torcello
Tel. +39 041 730119 (Call to check opening times)

Skyline Rooftop Bar Hilton Molino Stucky
Giudecca 810
Tel. +39 041 2723311
www.skylinebarvenice.com

A.S.D. Volavenezia
Aeroporto "G. Nicelli"
Via R. Morandi 9
30126 Venezia Lido
Tel. +39 041 3197061
www.volavenezia.org

Get Dressed! We're Going Out! Music and Theater

A concert in a charming *palazzetto*, a comedy by Goldoni, or an avant-garde stage show, some dancing in a tiny night-club? Venice offers endless possibilities for a special evening out.

For a sublime experience of French romantic music, surrounded by breathtaking stucco works by Abbondio Stazio and frescoes by Sebastiano Ricci, the rich concert program of the **Palazzetto Bru Zane – Centre de musique romantique française** is perfect. Built between 1695 and 1697, the Palazzo Zane casino, since 2009, is once again dedicated to music, its original vocation.

Commedia dell'Arte, Venetian traditional theater, but also experimental plays are the focus of the smallest theatre in Venice, the **Teatro a L'Avogaria**. Founded by Giovanni Poli in 1969, the theater also has an acting school whose best students have become members of the Compagnia Stabile.

Facing the north lagoon, in a fascinating brick and wooden structure, the **Teatro Fondamenta Nuove** is *"the"* contemporary place today in Venice, a space where theatre, music and dance can fully express their creative potential.

Finally, a drink at **Piccolo Mondo** is a must. Created in 1963 as an exhibition venue, it soon became a meeting place for artists from all the world: Peggy Guggenheim loved to come here and suggested the name "El Souk". Since 1978 it has been a unique nightclub that is still a main player on the Venetian night scene.

SIMPLE PLEASURES

Palazzetto Bru Zane
Centre de musique romantique française
San Polo, Campiello del Forner o Marangon 2368
Tel. +39 041 5211005
Free guided tours every Thursday. See website for details and times.
www.bru-zane.com

Teatro a L'Avogaria
Dorsoduro, Corte Zappa 1617
Tel. +39 041 5206130
www.teatro-avogaria.it

Teatro Fondamenta Nuove
Cannaregio,
Fondamente Nove 5013
Tel. +39 041 5224498
www.teatrofondamentanuove.it

Piccolo Mondo by El Souk
Dorsoduro, Calle Contarini Corfù 1056/A
Tel. +39 041 5200371
www.piccolomondo.biz

The Secret Message of the Bridge

The Borgoloco Pompeo Molmenti Bridge, near the Campo Santa Maria Formosa, is lined by elegant wrought-iron balustrades decorated by sinuous scrolls in the form of hearts. If you look very carefully, however, the pattern will reveal its secret message. The intricate decoration of this bridge, built during the Austrian occupation of Venice, in fact conceals the letters *W*, *V* and *E*, which stand for the patriotic cry "Viva Vittorio Emanuele".

A Day of Meditation

A stay on the lagoon can also be a quiet moment to find oneself. Then, nothing could be better than to devote a day to silence and meditation.

For this, a visit to the **Monastery of San Francesco del Deserto** would be the first suggestion. According to legend, St. Francis of Assisi landed on this tiny island in 1220 during a violent thunderstorm while he was returning from the Middle East and the Fifth Crusade. He planted the sprig of a pine tree there that soon grew so great that it shaded the entire island. After the Saint's death, the island was donated to the Frati Minori by the Venetian nobleman Jacopo Michiel so that the monks might build their monastery there. From the thirteenth century, the island of **San Lazzaro degli Armeni**, located between Venice and the Lido, had been used as a quarantine area – it was therefore dedicated to St. Lazarus, patron saint of lepers. During the eighteenth century, the island was entrusted to a group of Armenian monks who restored the already existing buildings, added new ones, and devoted their lives to learning. The island soon became an important cultural centre. A place beloved by Lord Byron who studied Armenian there, the island boasts a museum, a famous printing press and a wonderful library with paintings by Palma Il Giovane and a fresco by Tiepolo. Nevertheless, it is the magnificent garden that offers priceless moments of solitude and silence with its

extraordinarily peaceful view of the lagoon.
Finally, how about trying a private yoga session, maybe in a park? The vast green areas of the Sant'Elena Park, as well as the romantic Villa Groggia, are ideal locations in spring and summer to begin this discipline with your own personal yoga teacher.

San Francesco del deserto
Isola di San Francesco del deserto
Tel. +39 041 5286863
http://www.sanfrancescodeldeserto.it
Note: There is no public transportation to the island, which is accessible only by taxi or private boat. Don't forget a mosquito repellent in the summer!!!!

San Lazzaro degli Armeni
Isola di San Lazzaro
degli Armeni
Tel. +39 041 5260104
www.mekhitar.com
Note: The island can be reached with Actv line 20 that departs from the San Zaccaria stop at 3.10 pm.

Centro Yoga Dharma
Via Napoli 52
30172 Mestre (VE)
Tel. +39 041 5311954
www.yogadharmamestre.it

A "Liberty" Aperitivo

During the first half of the twentieth century, the Lido di Venezia was simply the most elegant beach destination in Europe. The first famous figure to fall in love with the Lido was Lord Byron, who went riding over its sandy dunes. Yet just a few decades later, this island, that during the Serenissima had served as a bulwark against the sea or potential enemy attacks, underwent a great transformation: the muddy and insalubrious creeks were reclaimed, and elegant gardens and streets lined with trees were created, with hotels and villas built in an eclectic mix of styles. These blended Gothic and Byzantine revival details with the emerging Art Nouveau, or Liberty, architectural style.

Architects and artists such as Nicolò Spada, who designed the Hotel Excelsior, as well as Brenno Del Giudice and Guido Cadorin enriched these buildings with turrets, terraces and *liagò* (covered terraces), multicolored stained glass windows, marble *patere* (reliefs), majolica decorations, frescoes and visionary railings, many created by the "iron wizard" Umberto Bellotto. An Art Nouveau lover's ideal itinerary on the island must definitely include the **Villino Monplaisir** (1906), with its façade decorated in the "*Wiener Secession*" style (Gran Viale, Angolo del Gallo); **Villa Otello** (via Lepanto, 12), for its magnificent gate decorated with peacocks designed by Bellotto; the sophisticated **Villino Gemma**, 1905-06 (via Dardanelli, 22); and the romantic **Villino delle Fate** ("Villa of the Fairies") built in 1914 (via Dardanelli, 50). The splendidly ethereal *berceau* of the **Villa Madonna** is located at the corner of Via Zara and Via Zeno, though the island offers magical and unexpected surprises at just about every turn.

To complete our exploration of the glamorous atmosphere of historical Lido, nothing is better than to have a drink at the **Grande Albergo Ausonia & Hungaria**. Inaugurated in 1907, this Old World hotel has still preserved original period furnishings and its terrace offers a magnificent view of the Lido's main street, the Gran Viale. Surrounded and charmed by the elegant majolica female figures and putti created in 1913 for the façade by Luigi Fabris, you will truly feel like you have stepped back in time.

SIMPLE PLEASURES

Grande Albergo Ausonia & Hungaria
Gran Viale Santa Maria Elisabetta 28
30126 Lido di Venezia
Tel. +39 041 2420060
www.hungaria.it

Beauties on a Bike

A warm summer day, when the air is still crisp and the sky clear, is a splendid time for a bicycle ride.

Bicycles are forbidden in Venice, but the 12-kilometer stretch of the Lido is just perfect to explore on two wheels. At the slow and relaxing pace of a bike, the Lido reveals its treasures: not far from the thirties-style airport, the Renaissance church of San Nicolò that witnessed the launching of the Fourth Crusade; the tree-lined seafront set along the beaches, with the Art Nouveau-style villas here and there, shining like precious jewels. Riding further on, the headquarters of the Venice Film Festival, the Palazzo del Cinema, the village of Malamocco, the Alberoni golf course…

For a sweet or savory break, the **Pasticceria Maggion** is a precious address: it has been baking unforgettable pastries and cakes, pizzas and quiches since 1958. During the Film Festival the renowned pastry shop becomes a glamorous and tasty gourmet stop for celebrities.

Not many people know that it is also possible to go biking on the island of Sant'Erasmo: bikes can be rented at **Il Lato Azzurro**. There, you are free to meander along vegetable gardens, vineyards and down the tiny streets of the island, breathe in the fine salty air, and make a stop to visit the Torre Massimiliana (1813). This massive imposing fortification overlooks the little beach called "Bacàn", a traditional hangout for Venetians. For a typical lunch, there is the **Agriturismo Vignotto**: home-made dishes made exclusively with local ingredients!

Lido di Venezia:

Noleggio biciclette (Bike Rentals)
Gran Viale Santa Maria Elisabetta 79/a
30126 Lido di Venezia (VE)
Tel. +39 041 5261490
www.venicebikerental.com

SIMPLE PLEASURES

Pasticceria Maggion
Via Dardanelli 48
30126 Lido di Venezia (VE)
Tel. +39 041 5260836
http://pasticceriamaggion.weebly.com/index.html

Sant'Erasmo:

Il Lato Azzurro
Via Forti 13
30141 Sant'Erasmo (VE)
Tel. +39 041 5230642
www.latoazzurro.it

Agriturismo Vignotto
Via Forti 71
30141 Sant'Erasmo (VE)
Tel. +39 041 2444000
www.vignotto.com

Murano... reloaded

Forget the image of sad little glass horses or pendants in painfully bad taste: the attentive visitor to Murano will discover secret corners and inspiring experiences.
Not far from the vaporetto stop Murano Colonna, which is the point of arrival to the island, you come to the glass shop **Giampaolo Nason** on the Rio dei Vetrai canal. The Nason family has been passing down the art of glasswork for more than six hundred years. Chandeliers, drinking glasses and figurines are handcrafted and made to order, thus making each piece an original.
A few steps on, you will come to the sixteenth-century Palazzo Contarini. This is home to the **Museo Barovier & Toso**, Venice's only private museum dedicated to glass. The more than two hundred objects showcased here are primarily the works of Ercole Barovier, who was one of the most important "entrepreneur-designer-artists" of the Murano glass world of the 1900s.

Continuing along the *fondamenta*, you won't want to miss the devotional art treasures preserved at the **San Pietro Martire** church. Upon request,

SIMPLE PLEASURES

you are admitted into the sacristy to admire the magnificent wooden altar frontals carved and sculpted by Pietro Morando. These works were brought from the Scuola di San Giovanni dei Battuti upon its demolition. Vestments and paintings that have been recovered from churches, monasteries and convents suppressed during the Napoleonic period are preserved in the adjacent **Museo Parrocchiale**.

In the nearby imposing **Basilica dei Santi Maria e Donato** an astonishing "zoo" awaits. The Basilica's pavement, that dates back to approximately 1140 a.d., is decorated with elegant mosaic work in marble and vitreous paste: broad entwined wheels called *rotae* are central to the nave, and in the free spaces, geometric motifs alternate with the depiction of animals of Persian-Sasanian origin: peacocks in couples drink from a cantharus, a heraldic eagle, griffins, dragons, two cockerels capture a fox (the cockerel and the fox also appear in the ancient Murano crest). This ancient and fragile "zoo of stone" is presently undergoing delicate restoration sponsored by Save Venice Inc.

And finally, as you leave the Basilica,

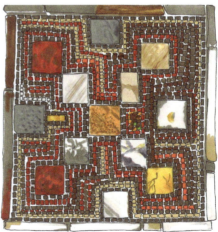

beyond the bridge, the genuine cuisine and spacious garden at the **Osteria al Duomo** will be just what you need after a day on Murano!

Giampaolo Nason
Fondamenta dei Vetrai 16,
30141 Murano (VE)
Tel. +39 041 739367

Barovier & Toso
Fondamenta dei Vetrai 28,
30141 Murano (VE)
Tel. +39 041 739049
www.barovieretoso.com

Chiesa di San Pietro Martire
Campiello Michieli
30141 Murano (VE)

Basilica Santi Maria e Donato
Campo San Donato
30141 Murano (VE)

Osteria al Duomo
Fondamenta Maschio 20
30141 Murano (VE)
Tel. +39 041 5274303
www.osteriaalduomo.com

For information on **Save Venice** activities:
San Marco 2888a
Tel. +39 041 5285247
www.savevenice.org

MY PRETTY VENICE

SOMETHING FOR THE HOUSE

"Velvet" Music

The rhythmic sound and steady, experienced movements of the women weavers are almost hypnotic. Still today, eighteenth-century looms continue to weave in this space suspended in time. These looms belonged to the Silk Guild during the Serenissima, and are today the pride of the historic family-run Venetian company **Tessitura Luigi Bevilacqua**. In 1970 they were used in scenes from *Anonimo Veneziano*, and are today the only looms of their kind in Venice. With musical "magic" and patient labor, for they produce no more than thirty centimeters of fabric a day, the looms weave an elegant collection of fabrics. These are not only for the home, but fashion designers such as Roberta di Camerino in the sixties, and more recently, Dolce & Gabbana, have also selected them for their creations. Elegant brocades and fascinating *soprarizzo* velvets have been used to richly grace prestigious private residences and public buildings in all the world. They come in a kaleidoscope of more than 3500 motifs that retrace the history of the art of textiles. These range from the brilliance and sensuality of silk, to the gold splendor in the Byzantine and Sasanian themes, to the dignified motifs of the Renaissance, and the sinuous Art Nouveau fantasies or Déco geometries.

Tessitura Luigi Bevilacqua's recent partnership with Chiara Pizzinato Atelier brings together the uniqueness of the Bevilacqua textiles with the creative inspiration of a designer. Chiara Pizzinato's creations, inspired by the textures and colors found in nature, reveal her background in botany. The magnificent result of this collaboration may be admired in the Bevilacqua Pizzinato showroom. Here, the passion of two professionals is expressed in elegant dresses, obi, and coats, creative and versatile stoles and handbags: one-of-a-kind articles or limited editions, all distinguished by impressive quality craftsmanship. A visit here is a must!

Tessitura Luigi Bevilacqua
Showroom Bevilacqua Pizzinato
Santa Croce,
Campiello de la Comare 1320
Tel. +39 041 721566

www.luigi-bevilacqua.com
www.bevilacquapizzinato.com
www.chiarapizzinato.it
The Showroom is open by appointment only.

Highlight:
The Chiesa dei Gesuiti was the home of the guild, or *scuola*, of silk weavers and tailors from 1643. The inscription that we find today at 4877 Campo dei Gesuiti reads "SCVOLA D SAN CRISTOFORO DEL OFICIO DI ARTE / D TESTORI DA PANNI DI SETA RESTAVRATA / L'ANNO MDCCIV" and there are scissors carved into the lintel stone over two little windows nearby at 4881. Between 1725 and 1731, the interior of the Gesuiti church was decorated with a *trompe-l'œil* of marble inlay that imitates the traditional Baroque brocade damask motifs. Of admirable beauty: the sumptuous pulpit on the left wall adorned with breathtaking drapery in marble and the precious stone carpet of the high altar.

Chiesa di Santa Maria Assunta detta dei Gesuiti
Cannaregio, Campo dei Gesuiti

Does Lace Come from Seaweed?

Of course not... though the origins of lace often take us back to a romantic legend. Apparently, there was once a fisherman who had to leave for sea for a long time. He decided to give his sweetheart a beautiful piece of decorative seaweed, a specimen of the *Halimeda opuntia* variety, that people call the "lace of mermaids". The young woman, wanting to preserve the beauty of the seaweed when it started to wilt, got the idea of creating a delicate piece of lace with thread and needle.

Legend aside, the existence of lace, above all needle lace, was documented in Venice as early as the 1400s. The elegant embroidery points of *reticello* netlace were known as "stitches in the air" since they were created without a cloth support. This type of lacemaking was a particularly long and complicated process, and at times it was even executed in gold and silver thread.

Women from all social milieux made lace in the city. Lacemaking was a means for women of the common people to contribute to the family income, while noblewomen saw lacemaking as an elegant pastime, on a par with sewing, embroidery, painting and music. At least three *dogaresse*, the 'First Ladies' of Venice, were known for promoting this womanly art: not only Giovanna Malipiero Dandolo and Lidia Priuli Dandolo, but also Morosina Grimani were fervent patronesses of lacemaking. The latter even created a workshop in her palace to teach the craft to young girls.

The fame of Venetian lace continued to grow until the end of the eighteenth century. Then, with the decline of the Republic of Venice and changes in taste, lace lost its popular appeal. It did enjoy a real comeback in the late nineteenth century with the creation of the Scuola Merletti di Burano in 1872. However, even then, the caprices of fashion only a few decades later decreed another slow decline.

To discover the secrets of lacemaking, a visit to the "Galleria del Merletto

Antico Dalla Lidia" is a must. This is a private collection with dozens of historic masterpieces. Be sure to look for the handkerchief that belonged to Napoleon Bonaparte! After admiring the magic of lacemakers at work, and listening to them as they eagerly share the secrets of their fine craft, you will certainly not be able to resist buying some genuine Burano lace!

Dalla Lidia Merletti
Via Galuppi 215
30142 Burano (VE)
Tel. +39 041 730052
www.dallalidia.com

The Witch's Mirror

The convex mirror called the "Witch's Mirror" or "Witch's Eye" because of its ability to reflect a wider visual angle than a normal mirror, has been considered a talisman in the home ever since Antiquity. **Witches' Mirrors** were seen as early as in the frescoes of Pompeii's "Villa of the Mysteries", and were an important element in Flemish painting (perhaps the most famous example is Jan van Eyck's *Arnolfini Portrait*). The Witch's Mirror also appeared in Venetian painting, reflecting the seductive female figures in Bellini's or Titian's works.

According to belief, these mirrors were to be kept veiled to avoid being soiled by the gaze of an impure woman. They could also be used as a means for divining the future.

So, how could we resist a visit to Stefano Coluccio's mysterious studio-workshop to take home such a fascinating object? There, we find dozens of different models, each highly original, and all of them handcrafted with traditional techniques and materials. Stefano learned his craft within the family, from his grandfather Emilio Canestrelli, who was an engraver, and his mother Manuela. So, all we have to do now is choose which mirror will "keep an eye" on our home...

Canestrelli
Dorsoduro, Calle della Toletta 1073
Tel. +39 041 2770617
www.venicemirrors.com

Fabrics... in an Ancient Monastery?

How these textiles are produced has always been a closely guarded secret. The methods were invented by the splendidly creative and eclectic genius Mariano Fortuny, who was not only an artist, but also set designer, fashion designer before his time, and brilliant textile designer. **Fortuny textiles** are still produced today in the workshop-factory that Fortuny purchased on the island of Giudecca in 1921. This was actually located on the site of an ancient monastery. A traditional process bent to semi-industrial needs was patented by Fortuny in 1910. He used this technique to enrich his famous printed cottons with subtle silky vibrations, and precious gold and silver motifs that oxidized to create an elegant patina. This antique sheen enhanced his decorative themes, such as his fine reworking of the Renaissance, Byzantine and Gothic, and also some lucky "finds" in the factory archives, such as the "Girandole e Nuvole", that have been brought back in a recent collection.

A visit to the Fortuny showroom means experiencing all of the magic of Mariano's world. The many varieties of fabrics, all carefully arranged by color, from the traditional yellows and blues, to reds and neutral shades, but also with new nuances such as greens that turn to blue and the many golds, pinks and silvers, are all a feast for the eyes. They have also been recently used to create an elegant line of accessories and objects for the home: boxes, dishes, candles, umbrellas and a huge collection of notebooks for all your ideas... in the Fortuny style!

P.S. Don't forget to have a look at the showroom's garden, and the fantastic fifties swimming pool – truly a rarity in Venice!

Fortuny SpA
Giudecca 805
Tel. +39 041 5287697
www.fortuny.com
The Showroom and garden are open by appointment.

SOMETHING FOR THE HOUSE

Venice in Miniature

The noble art of the blacksmith was for centuries considered of prime importance in Venice. Blacksmiths, "fravi" in Venetian, were obliged to work for free when requested by the government of the Serenissima. Moreover, strict controls were exercised over their production of strategic articles such as iron hardware for ships, or for weapons. It was only in the 1700s that **wrought iron** began to be used for decorative purposes, with the creation of magnificent railings for city palaces and the villas along the Brenta. The creative inspiration of blacksmiths of the Serenissima attained new heights during the early decades of the 1900s through the work of the eclectic and tireless artist-craftsman Umberto Bellotto. In just a few years, he had created dozens of decorative works throughout the city, from the lamps of the Mercerie to those of Piazza San Marco, the rosettes in the entrance to the former Cinema Italia, and the decorations for the homes on Corte dell'Albero. This centenary tradition is today given new impetus by Primo Bollani. In the footsteps of his predecessors, he forges railings, gratings and also restores, or adapts ancient wrought-iron objects. But that's not all. In addition to his traditional production, Primo has started making original sculptures in iron and steel too. On his workbench laden with tools, veritable works of art, miniatures of Venetian monuments such as San Marco's bell tower, the Rialto Bridge, the Arsenal door, the lions of San Marco, gondola prow-heads, or decorative two or multiple mullioned windows, are all worked in attentive detail with the artist's personal touch that makes each piece unique. A true Venice in miniature to take home with you!

El Fero novo
Castello, Calle de la Fava 5567
Tel. +39 041 5289422
www.elferonovo.com

Decoration Whims

A vintage armchair, an antique glass vase, a piece of sculpture: the best souvenir of a visit is often a unique object that not only holds memories, but also brings new inspiration to the home.

In Venice, a little detour off the set shopping route often holds delightful treasures, such as the true finds that await at **Baule blu**: teddy bears, dolls and antique miniature cars that have "lived" but are still fascinating; modern-antique or design touches for the house, such as chairs, shelves, lamps and mirrors. Here, sixties and seventies Venetian glass beads are sold by weight and there is always an original selection of vintage dresses, with designer labels.

Just a few steps away, there is a little boutique with a fairy-tale name where liturgical vestments, Fornasetti fabrics, and linens embellished with intricate monograms are given new life as lampshades. These fabrics, often embroidered with precious metal threads or with beads or sequins, are carefully cleaned and restored, then mounted on lampshade supports. Every piece is therefore absolutely unique.

Cenerentola ("**Cinderella's**") is also a precious address for beautiful old lace, pearl flowers, vintage clothes and collector's antique fabrics.

The **Saverio Pastor** studio (visits by appointment only) promises to be just as inspiring. Here *forcole*, or rowlocks, are made. They are the key element on any typical Venetian vessel: every curve and edge of these objects, carved from a single piece of walnut that has been aged for six months, has a specific function based upon the physique and rowing style of the rower. It is precisely for its plastic qualities that the *forcola* is also admired as a form of sculpture. It is a beautiful example of an object that begins as a handcrafted item to attain an almost artistic expression.

The forms of the forcole are also the source of inspiration for the decorative handles of the grès cups sold at **Arras**. This is a workshop and boutique run by a social cooperative. Overlooking the picturesque Campiello degli Squellini, here you will find handwoven scarves, exclusive accessories, as well as highly original bags made with recycled sails.

The fantastic caprices of Bassano ceramic fill the **Rigattieri** shop: since 1929, monumental pumpkin-tureens try to upstage countless bowls, salt shakers, obelisks and table centerpieces in Baroque style. It's hard to choose from the dozens of dishes in ceramic with perforated intricacies that so resemble precious lace work!

The traditional almost life-size "Moretti" figures may be found at the master gilder **Miotto**'s shop where you will also find elegant mirrors, lacquered trays and adorable gilt *puttini*.

Il Baule Blu
San Polo, Campo San Tomà 2916/A
Tel. +39 041 719448

Cenerentola
San Polo, Calle dei Saoneri 2718
Tel. +39 041 5232006
www.cenerentola.eu

Le forcole di Saverio Pastor
Dorsoduro,
Fondamenta Soranzo 341
Tel. +39 041 5225699
www.forcole.com

Arras
Dorsoduro,
Campiello degli Squellini 3235
Tel. +39 041 5226460
www.arrastessuti.wordpress.com

Rigattieri
San Marco, Calle Frati 3535
Tel. +39 041 2771223

Gianfranco Miotto & Figli
Castello, Ruga Giuffa 4945/47
Tel. +39 041 5200365
www.indoradorvenezia.com

My Pretty Venice

SOMETHING FOR THE HOUSE

Cameo

The Last Dogaressa: Peggy Guggenheim

Peggy Guggenheim loved to be photographed on the Byzantine throne of granite in her palazzo's garden, surrounded by her beloved Lhasa Apsos. Witty, vivacious, and never lacking in self-irony, Marguerite, known to the world as **Peggy**, settled in Venice after some restless younger years. In late 1948, she selected the unfinished Palazzo Venier dei Leoni to be her

residence and the prestigious home for her art collection opened to the public in 1951.

The collection, consisting of works acquired during two brief yet highly intense periods during which Peggy was determined "to buy a painting a day", continues in the spirit of her New York gallery *Art of This Century*. It represents a vast range of contemporary avant-garde currents and artists, including Braque, Duchamps, Miró, Giacometti, Pollock, Mondrian, Kandinsky, Ernst, Calder …

A vibrant presence in the lagoon's cultural world, Peggy was a regular at the restaurant all'Angelo on Calle Larga San Marco, a meeting place for Venice artists. She treated herself every day to the luxury of rides on one of the last *de casada* private gondolas (today exhibited at the Museo Navale di Venezia) wearing the impossible, eccentric creations designed specially for her by dear designer friends such as Ken Scott, who had begun his creative life as a painter, thanks to her support. Peggy's earring collection was equally as legendary: hundreds of pieces, some perhaps even having belonged to Marie Antoinette, ranging from highly precious to simple ethnic curios, covered the walls of her extravagant bedroom. Peggy Guggenheim died in December 1979. Her ashes were buried in her palazzo garden where her beloved dogs had also been laid to rest. Yet, her personality remains very much alive in the environment where she lived. The memory of her eccentricity too – such as how she loved to sit in the sun on her palazzo terrace, wearing those famous "bat" sunglasses designed by neo-romantic painter Edward Melcarth. They are also sold in the Museum's shop after being recreated by the brand Safilo.

In recent years, the original core of Peggy's collection has been enriched by the collections of Hannelore B. and Rudolph B. Schulhof, Gianni Mattioli, and by the Nasher Sculpture Garden. The Peggy Guggenheim Museum also often hosts temporary exhibitions and organizes educational activities.

Collezione Peggy Guggenheim
Dorsoduro, 704
Tel. +39 041 2405411
www.guggenheim-venice.itz

SOMETHING FOR THE HOUSE

Getting a Taste of Venice

Bàcari and Ostarie Hopping

Sip an "ombra" ("shadow") of red or white wine, a little prosecco, or taste the typical Venetian "Spritz" cocktail while chatting with friends on a *fondamenta*. Or grab a quick snack or savor a variety of appetizers, a delicious *polpetta di carne* (meatball) or *mozzarella in carrozza* (literally "mozzarella in a carriage")… Going "*bàcari* hopping" is definitely what Venetians do for aperitifs, dinner, or simply to be with people – a "Happy Hour" before its time that dates back to the eighteenth century when it was described in abundant detail by Goldoni himself.

The *bàcaro* is a seemingly simple place, usually located on a little side street, off the beaten tourist tracks. Here you can have a drink and taste the countless varieties of *cicheti*, delicious appetizers such as *crostini di pane* or *polenta con baccalà* (polenta with cod), *polpette di carne* (meatballs, but also made with tuna), marinated anchovies, fried fish skewers, *sarde in saor* (marinated sardines), and a range of *salumi* (cold cuts) and *formaggi* (cheeses) just waiting to be sliced on their cutting boards.

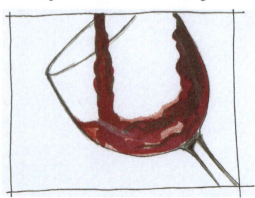

A few of these appetizers, a glass of wine or other, and you're off to the next stop. There, everyone continues eating, drinking, and talking, each time meeting new and different friends. At a *bàcaro*, the *cicheti* are served in stand-up buffet style, though a *bàcaro* may sometimes become an *osteria*. Then there will be a few places to sit and simple dishes can be ordered. Some *bàcari* also sell bulk wine, though perhaps it's a good idea to take your own bottles. It is not unusual to see the precious elixir being decanted into plastic mineral water bottles!

Every Venetian has his or her own list of favorite places. Here below are just a few suggestions, though of course there is no greater pleasure than discovering your "own" *bàcaro* !

Highlight:
The origin of the term "ombra" ("shadow") to refer to wine is interesting. It dates back to the days when the vintners on Piazza San Marco, to keep their wines cool, followed the great shadow cast by the bell tower as it turned during the course of the day.

Al Portego: *Cicheti in campiello* and "piccola cucina" (a few daily specials)
Castello, San Lio 6014
Tel. +39 041 5229038

Bacarando in Corte de l'Orso: Music, *cicheti* and also a vegetarian menu
San Marco, Corte de l'Orso 5495
Tel. +39 041 5238280
www.bacarando.com

Osteria alla Frasca: Picturesque pergola and Venetian cuisine in a quiet corner.
Cannaregio,
Corte de la Carità 5176
Tel. +39 041 2412585

Osteria Ca' d'Oro alla Vedova: Unforgettable *polpette*!!!
Cannaregio, Calle del Pistor 3912
Tel. +39 041 5285324

Osteria da Alberto: Authentic!!!
Cannaregio, Calle Giacinto Gallina 5401
Tel. +39 041 5238153
www.osteriadaalberto.it

Sottovento-Ostaria Serca e Sorsa: Excellent bulk wines. Look for the Coop supermarket, and Sottovento will be right behind you.
Riva Longa 27 – 30141 Murano (VE)
Tel. +39 041 5275385

Taverna del campiello Remer: Romantic in the evening, often with live music.
Cannaregio, Campiello del Remer 5701
Tel. +39 041 5228789
www.alremer.com

Un mondo di vino: A fantastic selection of *cicheti* in a former butcher's shop.
Cannaregio, Salizada San Canciano 5984
Tel. +39 041 5211093

The Dogaressa's Fork

It was Teodora, wife of the Doge Domenico Selvo (1071-85), and sister of the Byzantine *Basileus* Michael, to introduce various refined luxuries typical of the Middle Eastern courts. These included scented waters for the body, incense to perfume the palace interiors, but above all, she brought the predecessor of the **fork** to Venice. This was a curious two-pronged gold utensil with which Teodora brought food to her mouth. In this way, she avoided having to touch the food with her hands, though this was customary at the time. These extravagances were frowned upon by the Venetian people who later saw in the premature death of the Dogaressa the divine punishment for her "debauchery".

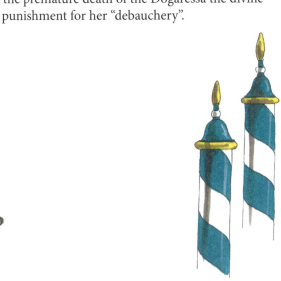

MY PRETTY VENICE

Spritz!!!

"Aperitivo" in Venice is synonymous with *Spritz*, a word that comes from the Austrian "Spritzen" and dates back to the time of the Austrian occupation. Then soldiers stationed in the city would water the local wine with sparkling water. The traditional Venetian recipe for Spritz calls for:

3 parts prosecco D.O.C.
2 parts Aperol
1 part soda

Pour the prosecco and Aperol in a tumbler filled with ice. Top with soda and mix. Garnish with a slice of orange and an olive.

GETTING A TASTE OF VENICE

Or, you can have a Spritz at:

El refolo
Castello, Via Garibaldi 1580
www.elrefolo.it

Caffè rosso
Dorsoduro, Campo Santa Margherita 2963
www.cafferosso.it

Al Marcà
San Polo, Campo Cesare Battisti, già Bella Vienna 213

Al Timon
Cannaregio, Fondamenta Ormesini 2754

L'Antica Besseta

There was once a little *osteria* run by a brother and sister. The man had a good heart and, once a week, offered the needy of the area a meal at half price, one *besso* precisely. The sister, on the other hand, was a greedy woman and a loan shark, and this earned her the nickname of the "Vecia Besseta". The *osteria* soon came to be known by the same nickname, though it was later changed to the present day "**Antica Besseta**".

The Besseta, off the beaten track, yet just minutes from Rialto, Piazzale Roma, and the Santa Lucia station, has tables for outside dining beneath a lovely grapevine pergola. It is located next to the narrowest calle of Venice, the Ca' Zusto, where it is impossible for two people to pass at once. Inside the restaurant, the atmosphere has kept all of its nineteenth-century magic. This is punctuated by period buffets and cabinets, marble-top tables, original Thonet chairs, and a collection of original paintings from artist habitués who have donated their works to the restaurant over the years. Here, traditional Venetian cuisine is creatively revisited. Its dishes always use seasonal ingredients: the homemade pasta, very fresh fish, unique sorbets are all accompanied by a selection of wines from an excellent cellar for an exquisite dining experience.

Trattoria Antica Besseta
Santa Croce, Salizada de Ca' Zusto 1395
Tel. +39 041 721687
www.anticabesseta.it

The Bride's Coffee

The scent of roasted coffee already titillates the nose dozen of yards away. Coffee has been roasted and sold here in the little *bottega*, located near the foot of the Ponte delle Guglie, since 1930. Heir to the coffee shops described by Goldoni's literary works ("*La Bottega del Caffè*"), the **Torrefazione Marchi-Costarica** was created by Signora Antonietta, precisely in 1930. She passionately ran the establishment until 1941, when the shortage of coffee caused by the war forced her to close.

At the end of the conflict, Signora Antoinetta's daughter Emilia opened for business again. She began roasting various qualities of beans daily just as her mother had done. These were all roasted separately to best enhance each coffee's aroma and characteristics. Since 2009, the *Bottega* has been classified on the prestigious listing of the historical houses and businesses of the Veneto. Here, among jute bags filled with beans from Guatemala, Costa Rica, Colombia, Brazil and Haiti, we can taste a delicious cup of coffee or buy one of the famous prized blends to enjoy at home. The most famous of these is "Caffè della Sposa" ("Bride's Coffee"), created by Camillo Marchi in the fifties. The prestigious coffee in fact consists of eight different kinds, with the proportions of the blend kept jealously secret. The invention of the "Bride's Coffee" is traced back to a certain young Venetian woman named Ninetta. According to the story, on the morning of her wedding day, she suddenly felt on the verge of fainting. Her mother came running to her rescue with a cup of coffee prepared with a blend created "especially for you from the roaster Camillo". The girl drank the coffee and sprang back to life again, so bursting with energy that she had no problem facing the most memorable day of her life... and that was the birth of the "Bride's Coffee"!

Torrefazione Marchi srl
Cannaregio, Rio Terà San Leonardo 1337
Tel. +39 041 716371
www.torrefazionemarchi.it

GETTING A TASTE OF VENICE

Chocotherapy!

There are times when chocolate is the only answer! And the synonym for chocolate in Venice is "**VizioVirtù**"!

We are instantly enveloped in the intense and intoxicating aromas that come wafting from the great counter of the boutique of master chocolatier Mariangela. Barolo Chinato, balsamic vinegar, Passito di Pantelleria, cigar tobacco: these are only a few of the flavors of her pralines. Tablets are also featured with Grand Cru chocolate in varying percentages of cacao of different origins, enriched with dried or candied fruit, glacé flowers, and pistachios, sometimes with accents of cinnamon or chili pepper.

In winter, VizioVirtù offers fragrant hot chocolates, and in summer, refreshing ice creams. And, then, there are the exquisite creations inspired by the magical and suggestive atmospheres of Venice and the traditional holidays: chocolate Christmas trees and boxes, Carnival masks that are often preciously trimmed with edible gold. Ancient and rare ingredients come together in modern recipes in Mariangela's open kitchen where customers have the chance to watch the various stages of production. Incidentally, the macarons, as well as traditional Venetian biscuit classics, are also delicious. Take a little break from that strict diet, and let yourself be tempted by an exquisite caprice at VizioVirtù !

VizioVirtù Cioccolateria
S. Polo, Calle del Campaniel 2898/A
Tel. +39 041 2750149
www.viziovirtu.com

GETTING A TASTE OF VENICE

Impade, Haman's Ears and Zuccherini...

...These are delicacies that strike our imagination and above all take us back to the history of Venice and its Ghetto, which was the earliest in Europe. The government of the Serenissima ordered the Ghetto to be built in 1516, when it was decreed that the local Jewish people should live in a specific area of the city. Until 1390, this was the area of the foundries (*geti* in Venetian, a word that the first arrivals, the Askhenazi Jews, pronounced with a hard "g"). The rich history of the Jewish population of the city is retraced at the Jewish Museum of Venice and the Synagogue, both of which are open to visitors, and the Jewish gastronomic traditions are also kept alive in the city, for example, through the delicious production of the **Panificio Giovanni Volpe**.

For over fifty years, in this tiny bakery at the entrance of the Ghetto, unleavened bread and sweets typical of the Venetian Jewish culinary tradition are baked daily according to rabbinic law. It's difficult to choose between the delicious *zuccherini* (pieces of shortbread sprinkled with sugar), *impade* (short crust pastry with almond and honey filling), *azzime dolci* (unleavened sweets flavored wth fennel seeds and decorated with grooves traditionally made by pressing a thimble into the dough), and *orecchie di Amman* ("Haman's Ears" that are made with short crust pastry and fruit or chocolate filling).

The origin of the latter pastry's name was a reference to a moving episode in the Bible. This was the story of how Esther, through her intercession with King Assuerus, saved the Jewish people from the extermination ordered by King Haman's prime minister. The Jews celebrated their salvation from this terrible fate by preparing these sweets. This custom is continued today, and these sweet "ears" are central to the Purim celebration (a festivity that takes place about the same time as Carnival). An interesting note is that these sweets are "parve", that is, they do not contain milk or any dairy products and some, such as the almond ones are also suitable for anyone suffering from celiac disease. So, truly everyone can enjoy these wonderful pastries!

Panificio Giovanni Volpe
Cannaregio, Calle del Ghetto Vecchio 1143
Tel. +39 041 715178
www.panificiovolpegiovanni.com

Highlight:
An absorbing chapter in the history of the women of the Venetian Jewish community is reflected in the various "ketubah", or Jewish marriage contracts, exhibited at the **Museo Ebraico (Jewish Museum)**. Written upon precious parchment scrolls, these marriage contracts described in detail the economic, social and marital obligations of the husband to his wife, so that woman's rights in case of divorce would be defended.

Museo Ebraico di Venezia
Cannaregio, Campo del Ghetto 2902\b
Tel. +39 041 715359
www.museoebraico.it

Rings...to Eat?

Typical delicious biscuits, *golosessi*, pastries and sweets of Venice and the lagoon abound, but the **bussolà buranelli** are definitely the most famous and loved. Traditionally made during the Easter season on the colorful island of Burano, they were prepared in every family according to a recipe handed down from mother to daughter for generations (so that explains why they are found everywhere!). The dough was shaped into biscuits in the form of a ring or the letter "S", then taken to the communal "forno" (oven) on the island to be baked. Once the biscuits were baked, they wonderfully smelled of butter, vanilla and lemon and were then kept in wardrobes where, for months, they would give a lovely scent to the linen. The rich and intensely yellow dough of the biscuits hardens over time, making the biscuits perfect to *mogiar* (dip) in sweet wine at the end of a meal.

Two special addresses:

Carmelina Palmisano
Via San Martino Destro 323 – 30142 Burano (VE)
Tel. +39 041 730010

Pasticceria Nobile
Cannaregio,
Rio Terà San Leonardo 1818
Tel. +39 041 720731
www.pasticcerianobile.it

GETTING A TASTE OF VENICE

If you want to make these biscuits at home, here's the recipe!
It is customary to make lots of **bussolà** at once, so invite your friends to enjoy some traditional biscuits of the lagoon!

Ingredients
1 kg White baking flour
350 g Butter
600 g Sugar
1 Egg
11 Egg yolks
1 Generous pinch of salt
1 Vanilla bean
Grated peel from one lemon

Method
Work the butter with the sugar and grated lemon peel together. Slit the vanilla bean in half, carefully removing the seeds. Then, add them to the butter. Beat the egg and the egg yolks in a bowl, and add them to the mixture of butter and sugar. Add the flour that you will have sieved together with the salt.
Mix the ingredients well. Pat the dough into a loaf and place in the refrigerator to rest for two hours.
Then, divide the dough into mounds of 100 g each. Shape each of these into cylinders of about 20 cm and then join the ends to form a ring. Bake in an oven at 185°C for 25 minutes, or until the biscuits are light golden brown. A variant would be to divide the dough into smaller mounds, say, of 30 g each, and shape each into an "S". These may be baked at the same temperature, but only for 15 minutes.

A Jewel to Sip

Dorona: the "Golden Grape" is a name that beautifully describes the intense golden nuances of this special vine with its grapes found only in the Venice lagoon area. Once prominent in all of the gardens of the lagoon, it was grown widely until the fifteenth century when it became almost completely extinct. That is, until 2002, when Gianluca Bisol, whose family produces prosecco, happened to see some Dorona grapes growing in a garden next to the Torcello Cathedral.
This discovery launched a fascinating "treasure hunt" that led to the recovery of approximately eighty Dorona vines scattered around the lagoon islands. Dorona vine cuttings were then planted in an ancient vineyard surrounded by medieval stone walls on the island of Mazzorbo. And thus the winery "Venissa" was born, a name inspired by Andrea Zanzotto's poem dedicated to "Venessia, Venissa, Venusia". It is in this "extreme" vineyard, immersed in a brackish climate and occasionally subject to the invasion of the high tide, that were harvested the first Dorona grapes in centuries.
Today, a visit to Venissa is an emotional journey appeals to all the senses at once. The sight is delighted by the charming panorama of the estate's vineyard, vegetable gardens and orchards at the foot of the ancient bell tower of the now vanished church of San Michele Arcangelo: the vegetable gardens are tended by retirees of Burano that carefully follow the dictates of the seasons. The sense of smell is enchanted by the fragrances of the multitude of cultivated and wild flowers and plants, while the hearing rests

in the suggestive, almost unreal peace that reigns in this very special place. Finally, taste enjoys the original and exclusive culinary creations to be discovered in Venissa's astounding restaurant, open from May to October, or in the suggestive Vinoteca, open all year round, overlooking the property's vineyard and the Mazzorbo Canal.

Venissa's high-concept restaurant offers a counterpoint to the cuisine of the Vinoteca, with its *cicheti* and dishes whose ingredients come fresh daily from the vegetable gardens or the local fish farm. Whether in the restaurant or the Vinoteca, the undisputed protagonists are of course the wines, veritable jewels for the palate: the **Venissa** and **Rosso Venissa**. The former, "the liquid gold of native Venice", is a collectible white wine. Rich and perfumed, it is vinified by the method normally used for red wines, that is, with the grape skins macerating for thirty days in the must, thus enriching Venissa with the strong tones of a red wine, yet the color and aroma of a white wine. The more recent Rosso Venissa, born from a grape planted on the Santa Cristina island by the Armenians more than forty years ago, is characterized by an intense red hue enriched by savory notes and the scents of salt marsh flowers.

Both wines are presented in Murano bottles designed to be authentic sculptures. These works of art reflect the essence of three ancient Venetian traditions: wine, glass and gold. The bottles, designed by Giovanni Moretti and crafted in the Murano ovens of the Carlo Moretti glass factory, are embellished with a gold-leaf label for Venissa, and a copper-leaf label for the Rosso. Both are handmade by Berta Battiloro, a descendant of an ancient goldsmith family.

Venissa
Fondamenta Santa Caterina 3
Isola di Mazzorbo – 30170 Burano (VE)
Tel. +39 041 5272281
www.venissa.it

Just Like a True Venetian

An Enchanted Evening: Carnival and the Doge's Ball

Described as "the most sumptuous, elegant and exclusive ball in the world..." and "one of the ten things you absolutely have to do in your life", the Doge's Ball is par excellence *the* prestigious social event of Carnival. In the past, during the Serenissima, Carnival was celebrated with private balls as well as public fetes. It was the time when everyone – nobility and bourgeoisie, commoners, and even monks and nuns – safely concealed behind those masks that liberated inhibitions, could indulge in all sort of pleasures. After the fall of the Republic of Venice, the tradition of Carnival was abandoned, and it was only revived in the late seventies. Then, in 1994, **Antonia Sautter**, approached for a BBC production, created the most magnificent and unforgettable masquerade ball ever: the Doge's Ball was born. Based on a concept developed by its eclectic creator, this event annually gathers about four hundred guests in the Palazzo Pisani Moretta, one of the most opulent palaces on the Grand Canal. The suggestive and often dream-like decors pay tribute to the traditions of the past, while embracing a new contemporary expression. They form the setting for the exciting performances of top-class international artists and the elegant theme dinner to the guests' spellbound delight. Indeed, they too become stars of the show, thanks to the spectacular costumes that they can buy or rent at Antonia Sautter's atelier: created with the designer's inimitable creative genius and craftsmanship, satins and velvets, organdie and damasks, adorned with ribbons, feathers, lace, shimmering beads, and Swarovski crystals, they enchant for the unusual chromatic balance and

JUST LIKE A TRUE VENETIAN

Antonia's extraordinary care in the details.
The breathtaking colors and nuances, together with Antonia's extraordinary attention to every detail, create sheer magic.
The Doge's Ball is quite simply an event without equal, an evening when dream and reality become one... and unforgettable.

Antonia Sautter Creations & Events
San Marco, Calle del Carro 1628
Tel. +39 041 2413802
www.ilballodeldoge.com

JUST LIKE A TRUE VENETIAN

Romantic Crusades: St. Mark's Bocolo

Once upon a time, during the dogado of Maurizio Galbaio, a young Venetian noblewoman by the name of Maria Partecipazio fell hopelessly in love with young Tancredi, a commoner. Since Maria's father and the Doge himself objected to this union, Maria suggested to her beloved to "ennoble himself" by going to fight against the unfaithful.

Tancred became a valiant warrior, but was fatally wounded, it was believed, at Roncesvalles. Before he drew his last breath, however, he picked a white rose from a nearby rosebush and dipped it in his blood, asking his friend Roland to take the flower to Venice. Maria received this extreme token of love on the 24th of April. The next morning, the feast day of the city's patron saint St. Mark, Maria was found lying lifeless on her bed, the rosebud that Tancred had sent to her held tight against her heart. As if by magic, the flower had sprung back to life again, as fresh as ever, and was a vibrant red. Since that day, every 25th of April it is the tradition for the men of Venice to offer their women, but also their mothers and daughters, a *bocolo*, or rosebud, in symbol of eternal love.

So, if you are in Venice at that time, ask for your **bocolo** and don't forget to taste the traditional "risi e bisi" prepared with the first sweet peas of the season.

This was the main dish of the State banquet at which the Doge and the Venetian aristocracy celebrated St. Mark and the coming of spring.

"La biondina in gondoeta"
(Boat Song)

The *biondina*, or little blonde, in the song by poet Antonio Lamberti was actually the noblewoman Marina Chiara Querini Benzon, famous for her tormented love life and the illustrious figures who frequented her salons. Figures such as Antonio Canova, Lord Byron and Ugo Foscolo were often hosted at her palazzo on the Grand Canal.

The "Biondina" is an example of the *canzone da batelo*, created as entertainment during the *freschi*. These were magical evening rides taken in gondolas colorfully decked out with balloons. The most sumptuous *freschi* consisted of a procession of boats around an illuminated *zattera* or barge, called "la galleggiante" upon which artists sometimes performed.

Marry me in Venice!

An unforgettable marriage proposal? Followed by an equally unique wedding? Or a special anniversary? Of course, in Venice!
Piazza San Marco and the Caffè Florian: two world famous names that make us irresistibly start to dream... Not many people know, however, that the historic café inaugurated by Floriano Francesconi on 29 December 1720 as "Alla Venezia Trionfante" ("To Triumphant Venice") – but immediately re-baptized by Venetians as simply "Florian" – offers an exclusive service called **"Marry Me!"**. This is a package totally devoted to sealing a romantic proposal, or the renewal of a couple's vows of love. You will experience a moment to remember seated in one of precious rooms of your choice, in the most beautiful and famous salon in the world, enveloped in the magical music of the Orchestra Florian. You will be pampered with skill and passion by the Caffè's staff, amidst chalices of bubbly and exquisite sweets.
And when the moment comes for the Venetian wedding of your dreams,

Will you marry me?

marryme@caffeflorian.com

JUST LIKE A TRUE VENETIAN

Vor that special anniversary or ritual celebration, let the "Fairy Godmothers" at the exclusive agency "Pretty Nice", see to everything. They are specialized in creating and organizing the perfect boutique wedding. Whether stylish or creative, ecological or traditional, *shabby chic* or designer, the weddings and events created by Pretty Nice are always absolutely "made to measure". They may be set in a romantic rococo palazzo or a contemporary space, an enchanted garden or a period yacht. (See *www.treschef.it*)

Confide your most secret desires to the "Fairy Godmothers" and – above all – let them know your budget! Then... sit back and relax, as the celebration you have always dreamed of becomes a moving and unforgettable reality.

Caffè Florian
Piazza San Marco 57
Tel. +39 041 5205641
www.caffeflorian.com
marryme@caffeflorian.com

Pretty Nice Weddings
www.prettynice.it
info@prettynice.it

A Queen in Venice?

No, Venice never had a Queen. The *Dogaresse*, or Doge's consorts, were kept from exercising any real form of power. Their role as "First Ladies" was basically a representational one, and their activities were closely supervised by the magistrates of the Republic.

There was, however, one exception: the Venetian-born **Caterina Cornaro,** who became Queen of Cyprus. Caterina was born in 1454, and her father's maternal grandfather was the Emperor John IV of Trebizond. In 1468, when Caterina was still just a girl, she was married by proxy to James II Lusignan, King of Cyprus. This was actually the result of a deal: the cancellation of a debt as part of her dowry of over 100,000 ducats. Cyprus was of crucial importance for trade and commerce, and this proposal was unquestionably to the advantage of the Cornaros and the Serenissima. Caterina departed to rule in 1472, when she became of age, yet only a year later the King died as a result of a hunting accident. Caterina, as Queen of Cyprus, nevertheless managed to stay in power until 1489. She finally abdicated when the Serenissima "proposed" that she surrender her kingdom in exchange for a fief in Asolo, in Venetian territory.

Caterina's return to Venice was met with grandiose celebrations that are still recalled today by the costumed parade that opens each annual Regata Storica held on the first Sunday of September. Caterina Cornaro's court at Asolo became an important circle of artists and men of letters such as Pietro Bembo, Giorgione and Lorenzo Lotto. Caterina herself spent her days either at Asolo or at the ancestral palace in Venice. The latter, rebuilt in 1724, became known as the Ca' Corner della Regina, and is today home to the Fondazione Prada.

Caterina died in 1510 and was buried in the church Santi Apostoli. Her remains were later put to rest in the church of San Salvador, where still today visitors may visit her tomb.

Fondazione Prada – Ca' Corner de la Regina
Calle de Ca' Corner, Santa Croce 2215
Tel. +39 041 8109161
www.fondazioneprada.org

Fresco in a Gondola and Costicine

For Venetians, it would be simply unthinkable to miss this event.
The Palladian Basilica di San Pietro di Castello was, until 1807, the seat of the Venetian patriarch. In the shade of the grassy campo in front of the Basilica, however, a lively program of events takes place each year in honor of Saints Peter and Paul. For over forty years now, the five-day fete becomes a carefree mix of religious celebrations and lay events: liturgical rites, live music, children's games, conferences, free guided tours of the Basilica, and exhibitions create a truly popular event that is also the expression of Venice's history and culture.
Local volunteer associations organize a small fundraising market selling bric-a-brac beside the church: curios, knick-knacks, old books, and also

delicious homemade sweets. The traditional puff pastries in the shape of a key, are the much awaited favorites of all the children, as are, of course, the balloons!

Midway along the walk that leads from the bridge to the Basilica, visitors will see a white stone. This marks the point where historically the Venetian patriarch, on his annual visits, would meet the Doge... It is also where today we stand in lines (often rather long!) for the gastronomic cuisine stands. The dishes are simple and typically Venetian: fried fish, polenta with *costicine* (ribs) and sausages, pasta and beans, *bigoli in salsa* – all to the generous flow of white wine. Sit at one of the long wooden tables, or on the grass, or with your feet happily dangling over the canal!

After dinner, you are welcome to take part in a **fresco**. The local rowing associations offer magic rides in illuminated gondolas around the ramparts of the ancient Arsenal. Before you leave (usually after a few traditional sprinkles of rain during the evening concert), treat yourself to a T-shirt to remember the fete and a magical summer's evening.

For information:
www.sanpierodecasteo.org

The "Famosissima" Night: Il Redentore

The enchanting midsummer celebration **Il Redentore** ("The Redeemer") recalls the end of the Plague that struck the Serenissima from 1575 to 1577 and this event is still today considered by Venetians their most moving religious holiday.

The epidemic, brought on Venetian vessels from the Orient together with the precious loads of spices and other products, was of unprecedented virulence. It took the lives of more than 50,000 people, with among the victims such illustrious figures as the painter Titian. As fires were being lit with branches of juniper to purify the air in the city, the government exhorted the population to pray fervently for the end of the scourge, and it made a solemn vow to build a new church dedicated to the Redentore. The first stone of this church was laid on 3 May 1577 on the island of Giudecca. During the following July, it was decided that the third Sunday of that month would forever be dedicated to a pilgrimage to the Redentore, and that it would be made across a bridge formed of boats from Piazza San Marco to the Giudecca.

Soon, a custom among the people developed alongside this religious tradition. Though popular, it was profoundly meaningful: on the occasion of the Feast, the houses of the Giudecca were repainted and decorated, and the faithful, after the pilgrimage, lingered on the banks of the island, eating and toasting. The banks too started to be decorated with fronds, flowers and *balòni*, colorful paper balloons, lit from the inside with a candle. Against this backdrop, a fireworks show brought the celebration to a close.

Even today, in memory of the ancient vow and tradition, thousands of Venetians make the pilgrimage to the Redentore over the bridge made of boats. On the eve of the Feast a most moving moment occurs. Then, joyous tables decorated with lights and festoons crowd the banks overlooking the Bacino di San Marco (Bay) and fill the adjacent campi

JUST LIKE A TRUE VENETIAN

and calli. In the Bay, hundreds of boats gather, carrying tables and chairs, with their groups of family and friends. At sunset, dinner begins: *bigoli in salsa, anara col pien, pasta e fasoi, sarde in saor,* big watermelons kept cool in a tub of water, white and red wine flowing freely. Suddenly, at 11:30 pm, an explosion: it's the fireworks show. Silence falls over the Bay, and for over a half an hour, the *foghi* reign supreme. The sky is ablaze with pure magic, the dazzling choreography of the fireworks is echoed in the reflections of the lagoon in a deafening crescendo. Suddenly, three explosions in quick succession mark the end of the show. The boats slowly pull out, one after the other, and start home... Or, they may set out in the direction of the Lido, where celebrations continue on the beach, amidst singing, bonfires and midnight swims.

JUST LIKE A TRUE VENETIAN

In Tintoretto's Studio

The tall narrow Gothic building at 3399 along the picturesque Fondamenta dei Mori, in the Cannaregio sestiere, was where the painter Jacopo Robusti, better known as Tintoretto, and his big family lived. Just a few meters away, if you look out for a rustic bench surrounded by terracotta pots with lavender, geranium and jasmin, this will be the artistic printshop, **Bottega del Tintoretto**. The studio, in activity since 1986, is equipped with presses recovered from ancient Venetian printshops. There is even a lithographic press dating back to 1890 and the *Bottega* is committed to preserving and promoting the tradition of artisan printmaking. Here it is possible to produce artistic prints with traditional and experimental techniques, and also draw upon the precious experience of a master printer in the production

This mysterious inscription on the lintel of Tintoretto's house has been variously interpreted as "n(ec) tecum nec s(i)n(e)te", most probably the abbreviated transcription of Ovid's famous quote from his Amores, "So I can't live either without you or with you".

of complete print runs. The works that artists have created here cover the walls of the printshop and, almost like a tutelary deity, the presence of Tintoretto himself seems to hover in the air. Indeed, monographs, publications and a range of documentation on the great artist's work have been collected and may be viewed here.

To have the inspiring experience of working in a real Venetian art *bottega*, the studio not only offers annual courses in engraving and xylography, but also intensive summer courses: a five-day seminar on the basics of printmaking, drawing, and watercolor painting, as well as sculpture and binding. Master craftsmen and students of all ages and countries, have the opportunity of working and eating together (lunch is included!), often having their meals right on the *fondamenta*.

La Bottega del Tintoretto
Cannaregio, Fondamenta dei Mori 3400
Tel. +39 041 722081
www.tintorettovenezia.it

Cameo

Women Painters of the Serenissima

Venice has always nurtured great artists and has cultivated the extraordinary talents of women painters such as **Marietta Robusti** and **Rosalba Carriera**. Here were two artists who expressed with splendid grace the painting tradition of the lagoon, seductively capturing its emotions and colors. It is not surprising that both were, above all, portrait artists. They infused their works with womanly introspection and empathy, and both painters became phenomenally successful. Marietta Robusti (1560-1590) was the eldest daughter of Jacopo Tintoretto, better known as Tintoretto. She was an illegitimate

MARIE TINTORET.

child, but greatly loved by her father. Indeed, historian Carlo Ridolfi relates that Tintoretto considered Marietta 'the most cherished delight of his genius'. From a young age, Marietta enjoyed the privilege of having her own father as master in the studio. As a girl, he took her everywhere with him, even to see his clients, and she would be dressed in boy's clothes so as not to look out of place. Later, as a portrait artist, Marietta's own works were in such great demand that Venetian noblewomen vied fiercely to pose for one of her portraits. Word of Marietta's gift even reached the courts of King Philip II of Spain, and the Holy Roman Emperor Maximilian II of Austria. Though she was invited to be painter at court, in 1578 her father arranged for his daughter to marry a Venetian jeweler of German origin, Marco Augusta. She had a son from this union, Jacometto. The infant died at a very young age, however, and Marietta never recovered from the loss, she too passing away at the age of only thirty. "La Tintoretta", as she was affectionately known, was buried in the church of Madonna dell'Orto, not far from Tintoretto's masterpiece "Presentation of the Virgin in the Temple". The artist was inspired by his beloved daughter in this painting of the Virgin Mary as a little girl. Tintoretto was shattered by Marietta's death, and dressed in mourning for the rest of his life.

About a century later, Rosalba Carriera (1673-1757) was born, she too into an artistic family: her father was the son of a painter, and her mother a gifted lacemaker. Rosalba began creating patterns for embroidery and lace, and decorated fans. She first became known for her elegant miniature portraits on snuffboxes and soon began to paint on ivory. She loved ivory for the warmth that it brought to her small portraits of ladies: it was precisely her "Fanciulla con colomba" on ivory that gained her membership into the Accademia di San Luca of Rome in 1705.

Rosalba was an impassioned portrait painter and her success grew prodigiously. She chose to use pastels, a rare technique for portraiture, and suffused flesh with vaporous luminosity, as she delved with benevolent realism into the faces, characters and expressions of her subjects. Rosalba's home and studio became a salon where nobility and illustrious figures from all of Europe mingled with her fellow artists, painters, singers, and composers. Feted in Modena, Paris, and Vienna, the King of Poland, Augustus III, gathered more than one hundred of her works, and those of her pupils, in a collection in the Dresden Royal Palace, the famous "Rosalba Cabinet". From the age of seventy, however, Rosalba's sight progressively began to fail, and blindness took its toll on her health and lucidity.

She died on 15 April 1757.

The house where Marietta Robusti lived and worked is located on the Fondamenta dei Mori, Cannaregio 3399. Rosalba Carriera lived in the Casa Biondetti on the Grand Canal, near San Vio, and the façade of the house bears a commemorative stone.

Seduce Me Tonight...

In just a few exhilarating steps you are at the Peggy Guggenheim Collection, the Punta della Dogana of the Francois Pinault Collection, and the "exhibition in movement" presented in the museum dedicated to Emilio Vedova, in the Salt Warehouses. During the sixteenth century, the "Magazzini del Sale" were where the "Provveditori al Sal" in the Salt Office were located. The four Provveditori supervised the State monopoly over salt production and trading. And, it is precisely here that today *Ca' Maria Adele* is located, a veritable jewel of Venetian hospitality.

We are immediately struck by the astonishing style, one that borders on experimental fusion, of the Residence's interiors. This is expressed and developed in twelve sophisticated rooms and suites. Here, fine-tuned color harmonies, essences and furnishings all bring together sumptuous luxury and exotic and ethnic atmospheres in a brilliant evocation of Serenissima's history.

Ca' Maria Adele will seduce you: in 2013 it was named 'Most Romantic Hotel in Europe' by the Johansens Condé Nast group. You are dazzled by the audacious Sala del Doge that gained the Hotel the 2014 classification "second most sexiest room in the world". The exotic atmosphere of the Sala dei Mori and the Orientale astounds and delights. Indeed, it awakens the senses

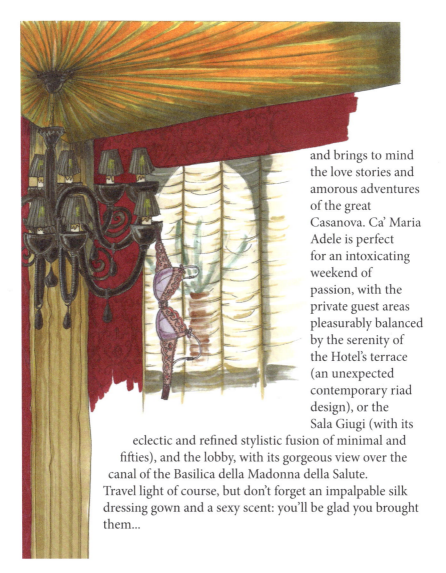

and brings to mind the love stories and amorous adventures of the great Casanova. Ca' Maria Adele is perfect for an intoxicating weekend of passion, with the private guest areas pleasurably balanced by the serenity of the Hotel's terrace (an unexpected contemporary riad design), or the Sala Giugi (with its eclectic and refined stylistic fusion of minimal and fifties), and the lobby, with its gorgeous view over the canal of the Basilica della Madonna della Salute.
Travel light of course, but don't forget an impalpable silk dressing gown and a sexy scent: you'll be glad you brought them...

Ca' Maria Adele
Dorsoduro, Rio Terà dei Catecumeni 111
Tel. +39 041 5203078
www.camariaadele.it

A Collection Hotel

The intense, exclusive essence of black pepper pervades the spaces of the fascinating and historically charged **Hotel Metropole**.
The strong bond with the past is further strengthened by the presence throughout the Hotel and into the rooms of astounding collections of antiques acquired by the Beggiato family over the years. A veritable passion of the Hotel's owners, each of the more than 2,000 pieces are sheer elegance: exquisite antique fans become rare jewels in infinite variations adorned with feathers, painted silk, or lace; the collection of evening or cocktail handbags dating back to the late 1800s right up to the seventies; or the other delightful finds such as precious calling card holders in materials such as mother-of-pearl, tortoise, ivory, silver. There are the amusing corkscrews in the strangest shapes, often embellished by handles that are in themselves true sculpture.
In such a residence, each room is of course a unique experience. They are all decorated with precious Fortuny and Bevilacqua fabrics, the prized silks and brocade velvets that evoke the historic textile and weaving tradition of the Serenissima. The rooms are furnished in a harmonious mix of rare Venetian eighteenth-century, Oriental, and Art Déco. Not to be missed: the exquisite tea ceremony presented from October to March in the special decor of the Oriental Bar. During the spring and summer, the Orange Garden, a perfect Mediterranean oasis of peace just a few steps from San Marco, awaits amidst the scent of jasmine and orange blossoms. Another date to remember: the annual "Fashion Design Made In Venice", an event promoted by Hotel Metropole showcasing the excellence of Venetian craftsmanship.

Hotel Metropole
Castello, Riva degli Schiavoni 4149
Tel. +39 041 5205044
www.hotelmetropole.com

JUST LIKE A TRUE VENETIAN

MY PRETTY VENICE

Lose Yourself (and Find Yourself Again) in the Labyrinth of Love

Green *Buxus sempervirens* hedges create a rare eighteenth-century divertissement tucked away in the impressive park of the Villa Pisani in Stra, just a half hour's drive from Venice.

The **Labyrinth**, a symbol of our unconscious desire to lose ourselves and then find ourselves again, was designed by Girolamo Frigimelica in 1720. It was a voluptuous amusement for the Venetian aristocrats who spent their holidays on the banks of the Brenta. In this seductive and provocative game, a lady wearing a veil or mask, stood on the belvedere of a little tower in the middle of the labyrinth. Knights challenged each other to be the first to reach their Lady first. Only the lucky one who could find

the right way through the labyrinth would have the honor and pleasure of revealing her identity.

This labyrinth was particularly admired by Gabriele D'Annunzio. Indeed, in his novel *Il Fuoco*, the author made this labyrinth the backdrop of the anguishing scene as Foscarina loses her way among the boxwood hedges and her lover Stelio hides and only laughs at her cruelly "... never coming out of hiding, like a faun lying in ambush".

In addition to the Labyrinth, the park has many other interesting features. Of particular note are the orange grove, the coffee house and the stables. During the summer months, you may also borrow a mat and basket for a charming *déjeuner sur l'herbe*.

Museo Nazionale di Villa Pisani
Via Doge Pisani 7 – 30039 Stra (VE)
Tel. +39 049 502074
www.villapisani.beniculturali.it

Note: The Labyrinth is closed from November to March. At other times of the year, it may be closed in case of bad weather conditions or high temperatures.

MY PRETTY VENICE

"WE LOVE VENICE"

Giorgia Caovilla

("O Jour" Shoe Designer)

"A perfect marriage of melancholy and romanticism, a city that never ceases to surprise and amaze me. I will never be able to say that I truly know Venice; each time I discover new calli, I lose myself among the lesser known alleys and admire that special light that illuminates the lagoon making it the most unique city in the world. Her sometimes brazen but always elegant beauty is for me, born and brought up so close to the Serenissima, a continuous source of inspiration. St. Mark's square at night, when the tourists are asleep and the city falls silent, the Giudecca where you can be swept away by the beauty of Palladio's Church of the Redentore. And then, Murano and Burano, with their picture postcard houses. From the colors of Carnival that fill the heart, to the Venice Film Festival, the glamour moment par excellence. If I want to escape reality for a couple of hours, I go to 'Marisa', at the Fondamenta San Giobbe. The menu is set by the first patrons of the day, those who arrive first decide for everyone else, and you are never disappointed. Home cooking, ten tables inside, fifteen outside. This is one of my favorite addresses when I'm in Venice for lunch or dinner. Venice is a city of water, synonymous with creativity, luxury, and history. She is like a most beautiful Lady who never ceases to astound us. I dedicated a collection of my label 'O Jour', that I especially love, to Venice. I wished to celebrate the glamour of the Caffè Florian, the first café open to women. This I did by designing a shoe with a light, wide bow that, from the heel, grazes the floor. In homage to the immense creativity and nonconformist taste of that most famous great lady and art collector who left so much to Venice, I was inspired to create a soft leather sneaker, then gave it a feminine twist by adding satin ribbons and romantic details, to make it perfect for every occasion.
Venice is magic, charm, and pure poetry."

www.ojour.it

"WE LOVE VENICE"

Manuela Pivato

(Journalist and Correspondent "Nuova Venezia", co-author of *Veneziani per scelta*)

Venice Under the High Tide

"The Lady should not take offence if mine is a meteorologically unstable, and not very politically correct, loving tribute. The Lady, I believe, is so rich in splendor and beauty that maybe she can accept that somebody will pay homage to her not for her dazzling history, but for her fragility, for her exposed vulnerability, for a surrender that smells of salt and mud. This can happen once, twice, ten times a year, with little warning and formidable consequences. Announced by the scream of sirens, this is the little, big war that the Lady has been waging for centuries without ever having been able to win one single battle, and that Venetians face armed with Wellingtons and wooden planks.

During those hours, when the canals lose their banks, palaces their vestibules, and bridges their lower steps, and when every stone becomes a bar of soap, every calle a gust of sirocco, and every square, or campo, a port; during those winter nights, when the sea stretches out its paw, the Lady suddenly returns to her aqueous state, dark and ancestral. With the frenzy of day blotted out, she goes back to her natural element and, perhaps, tacitly thanks the lagoon that comes to possess her and that, in possessing her, purifies her. If you want to know Venice as only Venetians know her – a city with no land beneath it – then just wait for the next high tide."

"WE LOVE VENICE"

Silvia Zanella

(Caffè Florian Marketing Manager)

"I have been working in Venice for eight years, but I became a resident of the city only a few months ago: Venice is a city so desirable and impossible that I am still incredibly moved just living here. Venice gives you that same feeling that falling in love with a fantastic man does, someone who makes you completely lose your head, but who is almost impossible to live with.
He's frustrating, complicated, you fight with him... but you desperately love him, and you keep going back to him, because it is only with him that you feel totally alive. It's an irrational, contradictory feeling of love/hate, war/peace, attraction/repulsion.
Venice brings you to terms with your most secret and conflicting feelings: the awe of a bright orange summer sunset in front of St. Mark's, and the anxiety of hearing the siren announcing the high tide on a grey winter morning. The joy and pride of living in the most beautiful and unique city of the world, and the horror of seeing her invaded and marred by uncontrolled tourism or rogue administration. In the end, however, you forgive her everything... especially at nightfall, a moment of peace, when the city truly embraces and pampers you. I love to take the vaporetto in the evening, and with the water lapping just as in a soundtrack, to peek inside the windows of the palaces on the Grand Canal. I love to bike at the Lido, along the dykes, between the sea and the brushwood; it makes me feel alive and free.
I love the bohemian feel that, over the past few years, is taking over the Giudecca. In the summer I find it fun to listen to the elders chatting alfresco in San Pietro di Castello. I love the Giardini and the Arsenale quarters because they represent Venice in all her authenticity and because it feels great to take a walk there or read a book. I love Cannaregio for its silences and the sacredness of the Ghetto. I love the tenacity and passion with which Venetians continue to celebrate traditional dates such as the Redentore, the Sensa, the Regata Storica, the Salute, San Martino... I let myself be lulled by the gentle sound of the Marangona, the largest bell of St. Mark's, which tolls at midday and midnight. It is the only bell that survived the 1902 collapse of

the bell tower. It is a survivor, just like me…
I now live in Venice: I moved here just less than a year ago, and the move coincided with the end of my marriage. A new life and a new beginning, because as Henri De Régnier once said, 'There is no other place that transforms or forges us so completely as this city, that helps us to become what we were meant to be'."

… MY PRETTY VENICE

Holly Snapp

(*Owner and Manager of the Holly Snapp Gallery*)

"As a gallery owner, I travel often. When I come home to my adopted city, Venice, I am still amazed by its extraordinary atmosphere of color, light, and ease. You step back into time as you step off the vaporetto, and I am so grateful to leave the 21st century behind – to exchange it for a world of saturated colors, shifting lights, sparkling water, tiny bridges, and enchanting canals – where the daily shop for food is a joy, not a chore.

Having lived here over 25 years, my life in Venice is now very small – concentrated on my gallery and our studio. Holly Snapp Gallery is located just off the glittering bustle of Campo Santo Stefano, one of the last bits of Venice not to have been invaded by upscale chain clothing stores, glass and mask shops, or touristy tat. Instead, we have antiquarian book dealers, fine wine merchants, bespoke jewellers, ravishing art galleries and elegant antique shops. Venetian linens and perfumes and trattorias, interior design stores, a vintage clothing shop and not one but two delicatessens – a real rarity in modern Venice.

Our house on the Giudecca, which faces out onto the vast sweep of the largest, liveliest, and most exciting canals in the world, is the studio of the painter Geoffrey Humphries, one of the most important figurative painters working in Venice today, who produces portraits, nudes, interiors and still-lifes which could only have been painted after a lifetime of absorbing the tones and hues of Venice. Sensual, psychologically acute, and saturated with light and colours – opaque, translucent, radiant, suffused, misty, and crystalline – his work is a compendium of all that Venice has offered the painter: they are quite simply paintings that could be painted nowhere else.

My favorite visit in Venice is to San Giorgio degli Schiavoni, the tiny scuola where Carpaccio's St George and the Dragon cycle is housed. This is a marvelous series of fairy-tale vignettes of an imaginary yet remarkably convincing evocation of life in the Oriental world of 15th-century Venice. You realize that it was created in a time when people really believed in dragons and basilisks and unicorns – yet the turbaned merchants and chatting scholars could have been painted yesterday. Only five minutes from San Marco, but hard to find and with odd opening hours (Mondays 2:45 pm to 6:00 pm; Tuesday to Saturday 9.15 am to 1:00 pm and 2:45 pm to 6:00 pm; Sunday 9.15 am to 1:00 pm), it is the

only scuola which has retained its original cycle of paintings commissioned from Carpaccio himself, and it is an experience you won't soon forget. I lose myself in the narrative of knights, dragons, and damsels set in a world of magical Eastern architecture and colors – with romantic lighting and magnificent gilt, it's a step into a vanished world of marvels and miracles."